Travel Guide To

Frankfurt, GERMANY

Unveiling a City of Contrasts: Experience One of the Best of Europe's Most Vibrant Destination!

Wybikes Hinton

COPYRIGHT NOTICE

This publication is copyright protected. This is only for personal use. No part of this publication may be, including but not limited to, reproduced, in any form or medium, stored in a data retrieval system or transmitted by or through any means, without prior written permission from the Author / Publisher.

Legal action will be pursued if this is breached.

DISCLAIMER

Please note that the information contained within this document is for educational purposes only. The information contained herein has been obtained from sources believed to be reliable at the time of publication. The opinions expressed herein are subject to change without notice.

Readers acknowledge that the Author / Publisher is not engaging in rendering legal, financial or professional advice. The Publisher / Author disclaims all warranties as to the accuracy, completeness, or adequacy of such information.

The Publisher assumes no liability for errors, omissions, or inadequacies in the information contained herein or from the interpretations thereof. The publisher / Author specifically disclaims any liability from the use or application of the information contained herein or from the interpretations thereof.

TABLE OF CONTENT

Copyright Notice
Disclaimer
Table of Content
Introduction
Welcome To Frankfurt, Germany!

Overview of Frankfurt

Historical Background

Geographical Features

Climate and Ideal Time to Visit

Cultural Significance

City Layout and Districts

    Chapter 1
    Getting to Frankfurt

Airports & Flights

Train and Bus Services

Car Rental and Driving Tips

Public Transportation Options

Navigating Frankfurt's Public Transportation

Travel Safety Tips

Conclusion

    Chapter 2
    Transport and Getting Around

Public Transportation System

U-Bahn, S-Bahn

Tramways and buses

Tickets and fares

Biking in Frankfurt

Safety Tips

Car Rental and Driving Tips

Driving In Frankfurt

Taxis and Ridesharing

Walking Tours

Guided walking tours

Access for Disabled Travelers

Airport Transfers

Conclusion

Chapter 3
Accommodation in Frankfurt

Overview of Accommodation Options

Luxury Hotels

Budget-Friendly Hotels

Boutique Hotels

Hostels

Unique stays (apartments, serviced residences)

Top Recommended Hotels and Resorts

Choosing the Right Accommodation for You

Booking Tips & Tricks

Conclusion

Chapter 4
Top Tourist Attractions

Römer & Römerberg

Frankfurt Cathedral

The Städel Museum

Palmengarten

Goethe House

Main Tower

Senckenberg's Natural History Museum

Conclusion

Chapter 5
Exploring the Old Town

Historical Landmarks

Museums & Galleries

Traditional Markets

Walking Tours

Riverside Walks

Architectural Highlights

Cultural Centres

Conclusion

Chapter 6
Modern Frankfurt

Financial Districts and Skyscrapers

Contemporary Art and Architecture

Modern Parks and Recreation Areas

High-Tech and Innovation Centres

Urban Development Projects

Conclusion

Chapter 7
Cultural Experiences

Traditional Festivities and Events

Local Music and Dance

Art Gallery and Studio

Theatre and Performing Arts

Culinary Experiences and Classes

Cultural Tours and Workshops

Libraries & Literature

Conclusion

Chapter 8
Daytrips from Frankfurt

Heidelberg

Mainz

Wiesbaden

The Rhine Valley

Darmstadt

Taunus Mountains

Aschaffenburg

Conclusion

Chapter 9
Family-Friendly Activities

Zoos and Animal Parks

Amusement and Theme Parks

Interactive Museums

Parks and Playgrounds

Family-friendly Restaurants

Children-Friendly Events and Festivals

Conclusion

Chapter 10
Food and Dining

Traditional Frankfurt Cuisine

Best Restaurants and Cafes

Street Food & Local Markets

Wine & Beer Tasting

Vegetarian and Vegan Options

Food Festivals

Cooking Classes

Conclusion

Chapter 11
Shopping in Frankfurt

Local Markets and Bazaars

Shopping Malls and Centres

Souvenir Shops

Designer Boutiques

Antiques and Collectibles

Bookstores and Specialty Shops

Conclusion

Chapter 12
Nightlife & Entertainment

Bars & Pubs

Nightclubs and Dance Venues

Live Music and Concerts

Theatres and Cinemas

Casinos & Gaming

Evening Cruises

Comedy and Cabaret

Conclusion

Chapter 13
Wellness and Relaxation

Spa and Wellness Centres

Hot Springs & Thermal Baths

Yoga and Meditation Retreats

Wellness Resorts

Beauty Treatments and Salons

Relaxation Spots

Fitness Centres and Gymnasiums

Conclusion

Chapter 14
Sport and Outdoor Activities

Golf Courses

Horseback Riding

Sailing and Boating

Fishing Spots

Tennis and Sport Clubs

Hiking and Bike Trails

Water Sports and Activities

Conclusion

Chapter 15
Events & Festivals

Annual Festivals

Music and Arts Festivals

Cultural and historical Celebrations

Food and Beverage Festivals

Sporting Events

Seasonal Events

Special Interest Events

Conclusion

Chapter 16
Historic Sites

Römer & Römerberg

Frankfurt Cathedral

Goethe House

Archaeological sites

Historic Churches and Cathedrals

Museums & Exhibitions

Conclusion

Chapter 17
Itinerary and Sample Plans

Weekend Getaway

Cultural Immersion

Outdoor Adventure

Family-friendly Trip

Budget Travel

Luxury Experience

Conclusion

Chapter 18
Practical Information

Currency & Banking

Health and Medical Services

Emergency Contacts:

Internet and Connectivity

Postal Services

Travel Insurance and Safety

Final Thoughts

Chapter 19
Local Etiquette and Customs

Greeting and Interaction

Dinner Etiquette

Dress Code

Tipping Practices

Public Behavior

Respecting Local Traditions

Environmental Guidelines

Conclusion

Chapter 20
What to Do and Not Do in Frankfurt

Local Etiquette and Customs

Safety Tips

Environmental Guidelines

Common Tourist Mistakes

Respecting Local Traditions

Tips for Responsible Travel

Conclusion

Chapter 21
Greenspaces and Parks

Palmengarten

Grüneburgpark

Frankfurt City Forest

Bethmannpark

Günthersburgpark

Nizza Park

Lohrpark

Conclusion

Chapter 22
Unique Experiences

River Cruises Along the Main

Wine Tours throughout the surrounding region

Cooking Classes and Food Tours

Hidden gems and offbeat attractions

Art and Graffiti Tours

Local Markets and Artisanal Workshops

Seasonal Activities & Events

Conclusion

Conclusion
1. Recap of Frankfurt Highlights

2. Travelers' Reflections and Testimonials

3. Tips for Your Next Visit

4. Staying connected with Frankfurt

5. Final words and farewell

    Appendix
    Useful Resources

Emergency Contacts

Maps and Navigation Tools

Additional Reading and References

Useful Local Phrases

Conclusion

Addresses and Locations for Popular Accommodation

Addresses and Locations of Popular Restaurants and Cafes

Addresses and Locations of Popular Bars and Clubs

Addresses and Locations of the Top Attractions

INTRODUCTION

WELCOME TO FRANKFURT, GERMANY!

Frankfurt, often known as "Mainhattan" because to its spectacular skyline and the Main River that runs through it, is a city that seamlessly combines the old with the new. After spending a significant amount of time visiting this dynamic metropolis, I've grown to love its distinct character, rich history, and lively cultural scene. Allow me to introduce you to Frankfurt and provide some insights to help you make the most of your stay.

Overview of Frankfurt

Frankfurt is Germany's financial powerhouse and fifth-largest city. It is known for its futuristic skyline, which is dominated by high buildings, yet it is also a city rich in history and traditions. Frankfurt provides a wide range of experiences, from the busy business center to the picturesque old town. The city is home to the European Central Bank, the Frankfurt Stock Exchange, and other international corporations, making it a major role on the world economic stage. Despite its contemporary exterior, Frankfurt maintains a strong link to its historical origins, with well-preserved medieval buildings and cultural treasures.

Historical Background

Frankfurt's history extends back over a millennium. It initially appears in historical records in 794 AD as a Carolingian royal seat. During the Middle Ages, Frankfurt grew into an important commerce and financial hub, hosting one of the oldest and most prominent trade exhibitions, the Frankfurt commerce Fair, which is still held today. The city's name, Frankfurt am Main, symbolizes its strategic location along the Main River, which has served as an important commerce route for centuries.

One of Frankfurt's most noteworthy historical periods was the reign of the Holy Roman Empire. From 1562 until 1792, Frankfurt hosted the coronation of the Holy Roman Emperors. The Kaiserdom (St. Bartholomew's Cathedral) in the old town hosted these spectacular celebrations. Walking around the old town, you can still feel the impact of these momentous events.

Geographical Features

Frankfurt is located in the middle of Germany, in the state of Hessen. The city is located on both banks of the Main River, which drains into the Rhine River farther west. The river not only enhances the city's aesthetics, but it also acts as a transit and recreational hub. The surrounding scenery is characterized by lush Rhine-Main lowlands, with rolling hills and vineyards in the adjoining districts.

The city is split into 46 districts, each with their own distinct charm and character. Frankfurt has a wide diversity of landscapes to explore, from the sleek, modern skyscrapers of the Bankenviertel (financial sector) to the charming, cobblestone lanes of Sachsenhausen.

Climate and Ideal Time to Visit

Frankfurt has a moderate oceanic climate, with mild winters and pleasant summers. The city's weather is affected by its inland location and closeness to the Main River, which helps to mitigate temperature fluctuations.

- Spring (March-May): This is one of the greatest periods to visit Frankfurt. The weather is pleasant, and the city's parks and gardens are filled with blooming flowers. This is also when numerous outdoor festivals and activities begin, making for an exciting time to explore.

- Summer (June to August): Frankfurt's summers are warm and pleasant, with average temperatures of 25°C (77°F). This is peak tourist season, so expect larger crowds, particularly around major sights and during events such as the Frankfurt Summer Festival.

- Autumn (September to November): This is another great season to come. The weather is still quite moderate, and the autumn foliage in the city's parks and neighboring countryside is breathtaking. The Frankfurt Book Fair, one of the world's largest, takes place in October and is a key draw.

- Winter (December–February): Winters may be chilly, with temperatures occasionally plunging below freezing. However, the festive season brings the city to life with Christmas markets, ice skating rinks, and holiday lights, making it a lovely time to visit despite the cold weather.

Cultural Significance

Frankfurt is a cultural hub, with a diverse range of cultures, arts, and intellectual activities. Johann Wolfgang von Goethe, one of Germany's most famous poets, was born in the city, and his boyhood house has been converted into a museum. The Goethe House provides an intriguing look into the lives and times of this literary legend.

The city's Museum Embankment (Museumsufer) is a cultural treasure trove, with a collection of museums lining the Main River. The Liebieghaus houses ancient sculptures, while the Museum of Modern Art showcases modern art. The Städel Museum, which houses a significant collection of European art spanning seven centuries, is a must-see for art lovers.

Frankfurt is also noted for its thriving performing arts community. The Alte Oper (Old Opera House) provides a variety of entertainment, including classical concerts and current theatrical shows. The city's unique cultural environment is celebrated via several events, including the Frankfurt Jazz Festival and the Museum Embankment Festival.

City Layout and Districts

Frankfurt's city plan combines ancient and modern buildings, reflecting its vibrant history and dynamic present. The city is separated into various districts, each of which offers distinct experiences.

- Altstadt (Old Town): The hub of ancient Frankfurt, with the Römer, a medieval edifice that has functioned as the city hall for almost 600 years. The Kaiserdom and St. Nicholas Church may also be found here, along with picturesque cobblestone lanes and classic German architecture.

- Innenstadt (City Center): This is the business quarter, with the lively retail street Zeil, high-end stores, and the landmark Hauptwache square. The MyZeil retail centre, with its outstanding modern style, is a shopper's dream.

- Sachsenhausen: Known for its historic apple wine taverns, Sachsenhausen is a vibrant neighborhood with a mix of old and new. The area's cobblestone pathways and ancient buildings provide a beautiful ambiance, while the Museum Embankment provides cultural attractions.

- Bahnhofsviertel: Once a shabby neighborhood, Bahnhofsviertel has evolved into a fashionable quarter complete with chic clubs, foreign restaurants, and a thriving nightlife. Its proximity to the major train station gives it an ideal location for visiting the city.

- Westend: This upmarket neighborhood is distinguished by exquisite residential structures, rich green spaces, and closeness to the financial area. It is home to the Senckenberg Natural History Museum and the Palmengarten, a lovely botanical garden.

- Nordend: A bohemian area with a laidback air, Nordend is known for its cafés, shops, and tree-lined streets. The Günthersburgpark in this region is a popular place for folks to rest and unwind.

Frankfurt's numerous districts, each with their own particular character, provide a rich tapestry of experiences to suit all interests. Whether you're exploring the ancient alleys of Altstadt, shopping in the busy Innenstadt, or partying in Bahnhofsviertel, there's always something new to discover in this exciting city.

CHAPTER 1

GETTING TO FRANKFURT

Frankfurt is one of Europe's major transit hubs, making it quite convenient to get to and around the city. Whether you arrive by airline, train, bus, or vehicle, the city's excellent infrastructure will ensure a seamless journey. I've spent a lot of time navigating Frankfurt's transportation systems, so I've compiled a list of useful tips and observations to help you plan your trip. Here's a full guide to traveling to Frankfurt and taking use of its transit choices.

Airports & Flights

Frankfurt is home to Frankfurt Airport (FRA), one of the world's busiest and best-connected airports. Frankfurt Airport, located roughly 12 kilometers (7.5 miles) southwest of the city center, is a significant international transport hub.

Frankfurt Airport(FRA):

Frankfurt Airport acts as a hub for several international airlines, notably Lufthansa, which operates numerous direct flights to and from cities across the world. The airport is separated into two major terminals: Terminal 1 and Terminal 2. Terminal 1 primarily services Lufthansa and its Star Alliance partners, while Terminal 2 serves a number of other international airlines.

The airport is well-equipped with contemporary amenities such as duty-free stores, restaurants, lounges, and free WiFi. It also provides a choice of transit alternatives to reach the city core. Upon arrival, you can take a cab, hire a vehicle, or use public transit to your destination.

For further information, go to www.frankfurt-airport.com.

Frankfurt/Hahn Airport (HHN):

Frankfurt-Hahn Airport, albeit smaller and farther from the city (approximately 120 kilometers/75 miles), is another alternative, notably for low-cost carriers such as Ryanair. Shuttle buses connect this airport to Frankfurt's main train station, however the trip takes around 1.5 to 2 hours.

For further information, go to www.hahn-airport.de.

Train and Bus Services

Frankfurt's central location in Germany makes it an important railway hub, with strong links to cities throughout Europe.

Train services:

Frankfurt Hauptbahnhof is one of Europe's largest and busiest train stations. It's an architectural masterpiece and a vital transportation hub for passengers. Deutsche Bahn (DB) provides a number of high-speed InterCity Express (ICE) trains, as well as regional and international services from here. Whether you're traveling to Berlin, Munich, Paris, or Amsterdam, rail connections are simple and regular.

Traveling by rail in Germany has proven to be quite efficient. The high-speed ICE trains are pleasant and timely, making long-distance travel simple. Tickets can be booked online via the Deutsche Bahn website (www.bahn.com) or purchased at the station.

Bus services:

Long-distance buses are a good choice for budget-conscious tourists. Companies such as FlixBus and Eurolines provide services to and from Frankfurt, linking it to other important cities in Germany and Europe. The major bus station is close the Hauptbahnhof, making it simple to switch between bus and rail travel.

For additional information about bus services, go to www.flixbus.com.

Car Rental and Driving Tips

Renting a car can give flexibility, especially if you intend to explore the neighboring areas of Frankfurt. Major vehicle rental firms, including Hertz, Avis, and Europcar, operate counters at both Frankfurt Airport and the Hauptbahnhof.

Driving Tips:

- Autobahn: Germany's autobahns are famous for portions with no speed restrictions. However, always follow stated speed limits and use caution in high-traffic zones.

- Parking: Finding a parking spot in downtown Frankfurt may be difficult and costly. Look for P+R (Park and Ride) facilities on the outskirts of the city, which provide cheaper parking and quick access to public transportation.

- Environmental Zones: Frankfurt, like many other German cities, has environmental zones (Umweltzonen) that need a green emissions sticker for your car. If you plan to drive in certain regions, make sure your rented car has this sticker.

- Traffic Rules: Germany has strong traffic regulations that include the usage of seat belts, no handheld phone use while driving, and the use of headlights in low visibility.

Visit www.europcar.com to book a car hire.

Public Transportation Options

Frankfurt has a comprehensive and efficient public transportation system managed by the Rhein-Main-Verkehrsverbund (RMV). The system comprises U-Bahn (underground trains), S-Bahn (commuter trains), trams, and buses, making it simple to travel across the city and adjacent areas.

U-Bahn, S-Bahn:

The U-Bahn and S-Bahn form the backbone of Frankfurt's public transportation network. The U-Bahn is made up of nine lines (U1–U9) that mostly service the inner city and suburbs. The S-Bahn includes nine lines (S1–S9) that link Frankfurt to adjacent towns and cities.

Tramways and buses:

Trams and buses supplement train services by offering easy connections around the city. The tram network serves central Frankfurt, while buses service locations that are not accessible by tram or rail.

Tickets and fares:

Tickets for public transportation may be purchased from ticket machines at all stations, tram stops, and certain bus stops. You may also buy tickets using the RMV app on your smartphone. Frankfurt is separated into tariff zones, so be sure you purchase the appropriate ticket for your route.

A single ticket for travel inside Frankfurt costs roughly 2.75 Euro, whilst a day pass (Tageskarte) costs around 7.75 Euro and provides unlimited travel on all RMV services within the city for one day.

For additional information about public transportation, go to www.rmv.de.

Navigating Frankfurt's Public Transportation

The public transportation system in Frankfurt is easy to use owing to excellent signage and regular services. Here are some suggestions to help you move around:

- Plan Ahead: Use the RMV website or app to plan your route and check timetables. The app gives real-time information on arrivals, departures, and service disruptions.

- Validate Your Ticket: Before boarding a train, tram, or bus, check your ticket at the blue validation machines placed at station entrances or platforms. Failure to do so may result in a fine.

- Look for Signs: Stations and stops are properly marked. Look for a green "U" for U-Bahn, a white "S" on a green backdrop for S-Bahn, and a tram emblem for tram stations.

- Use Maps: Most stations include maps of the full network, making it simple to travel and find your way.

During my stay in Frankfurt, I found the public transportation system to be dependable, clean, and efficient. It's a great way to get about the city and beyond without having to drive and park.

Travel Safety Tips

While Frankfurt is typically secure, it is always advisable to take care, particularly in congested locations and while traveling alone. Here are some safety guidelines to bear in mind:

- Maintain Vigilance: Be alert of your surroundings, particularly in congested areas such as train stations, marketplaces, and tourist sites. Pickpocketing may occur in various places.

- Protect Your Belongings: Keep your valuables safe and avoid flaunting pricey goods such as jewelry or gadgets. Carry your essentials with a money belt or a safe bag.

- Use Licensed Taxis: If you need a cab, only use licensed taxis. Official taxis are beige with a "TAXI" sign on the roof.

- Emergency Numbers: Learn your local emergency numbers. Germany's universal emergency number for police, fire, and medical services is 112.

- Travel Insurance: Make sure you have adequate travel insurance that includes medical emergencies, theft, and trip cancellations. It gives you peace of mind and financial safety when you're traveling.

Conclusion

Getting to and from Frankfurt is simple because to its well-developed transportation system. Whether you arrive by aircraft, train, bus, or vehicle, there are handy and efficient solutions to meet your needs. The city's public transportation system is broad and user-friendly, allowing you to easily discover everything Frankfurt has to offer.

You can assure a smooth and pleasurable vacation by preparing ahead of time, using trustworthy transportation, and following basic safety procedures. Frankfurt's mix of modernism and heritage, along with its accessibility, make it an ideal destination for all sorts of tourists. Enjoy your travels!

CHAPTER 2

TRANSPORT AND GETTING AROUND

Navigating Frankfurt is an adventure in and of itself, with a variety of transit alternatives to make seeing the city both convenient and entertaining. Whether you prefer public transportation, bicycling, driving, or walking, Frankfurt's infrastructure is geared to meet your demands. After spending so much time in this fascinating city, I've discovered the best methods to move around, and I'm pleased to share my findings with you.

Public Transportation System

Frankfurt has one of Europe's most efficient and comprehensive public transportation networks, administered by the Rhein-Main-Verkehrsverbund (RMV). The network comprises U-Bahn (subway), S-Bahn (commuter trains), trams, and buses, making it simple to go throughout the city and to other places.

U-Bahn, S-Bahn

The U-Bahn is Frankfurt's subway system, with nine lines (U1 through U9) that serve the city and its environs. The trains are contemporary, clean, and operate regularly, often every 5-10 minutes during peak hours. U-Bahn stations like as Hauptwache, Konstablerwache, and Willy-Brandt-Platz provide access to significant attractions and commercial centers.

The S-Bahn, on the other hand, connects Frankfurt to the surrounding towns and cities. With nine lines (S1 to S9), it's ideal for visitors looking to explore the larger Rhine-Main area. The S-Bahn trains are similarly regular and travel through central Frankfurt, with stops at significant hubs such as Frankfurt Hauptbahnhof (Main Train Station), Hauptwache, and Frankfurt Süd.

Tramways and buses

With ten lines that run through Frankfurt, trams are an excellent way to see the city. They're especially useful for short trips and provide a picturesque way to go around neighborhoods. I frequently traveled tram line 11, which runs through the heart of the city and offers spectacular vistas and easy stops.

The bus network supplements rail services by connecting places that are inaccessible by train or tram. Night buses (Nachtbusse) are provided for late-night transport, allowing you to go about securely after normal services have ended.

Tickets and fares

Tickets for all kinds of public transportation may be purchased via ticket machines at stations, tram stops, and certain bus stops. You may also buy tickets using the RMV app on your smartphone. Frankfurt is separated into tariff zones, so make sure you get the appropriate ticket for your route. A single ticket inside the city costs roughly 2.75 Euro, while a day pass (Tageskarte) costs approximately 7.75 Euro and provides unlimited travel for the day.

For additional information and to plan your travel, go to www.rmv.de.

Biking in Frankfurt

Frankfurt is a bike-friendly city, with a rising number of designated bike lanes and trails. Biking is not only an environmentally beneficial way to get around, but it also allows you to explore the city at your own leisure.

Bicycle Rentals:

There are several bike rental options accessible across the city. Call a Bike, offered by Deutsche Bahn, is a popular choice. A smartphone app allows users to hire and return bikes at a variety of places. I found the procedure simple and convenient, making unplanned bicycling journeys a breeze.

For additional information, go to www.callabike.de.

Bicycle Routes:

Frankfurt has a variety of picturesque biking paths. The Main River bike route is one of my favorites, since it runs along the riverbanks and provides breathtaking views of the skyline. The Grüneburgpark and Palmengarten areas are also ideal for leisurely rides.

Safety Tips

Wear a Helmet: While not required, wearing a helmet is strongly advised for safety.

Follow Traffic Rules: Cyclists must follow the same traffic laws as motor vehicles. Pay attention to traffic signals and road signs.

Use Bike Lanes: Wherever possible, use designated bike lanes to safeguard your own and other pedestrians' and vehicles' safety.

Car Rental and Driving Tips

Renting a car in Frankfurt can give flexibility, especially if you intend to explore the neighboring areas. Major vehicle rental firms, including Hertz, Avis, and Europcar, operate counters at Frankfurt Airport and the Hauptbahnhof.

Driving In Frankfurt

Driving in Frankfurt is pretty uncomplicated, although there are a few things to consider:

Autobahn: Germany's autobahns are famous for portions with no speed restrictions. However, always follow stated speed limits and use caution in high-traffic zones.

Parking: Finding a parking spot in downtown Frankfurt may be difficult and costly. Look for P+R (Park and Ride) facilities on the outskirts of the city, which provide cheaper parking and quick access to public transportation.

Environmental Zones: In Frankfurt, environmental zones (Umweltzonen) demand a green emissions sticker on your car. If you plan to drive in certain regions, make sure your rented car has this sticker.

Traffic Rules: Germany has strong traffic regulations that include the usage of seat belts, no handheld phone use while driving, and the use of headlights in low visibility.

Visit www.europcar.com to book a car hire

Taxis and Ridesharing

Taxis are commonly available in Frankfurt and may be hailed on the street, located at taxi stands, or booked over the phone. Official taxis are beige with a "TAXI" sign on the roof.

Taxi services:

MyTaxi (now free): This app-based service lets you order and pay for cabs from your smartphone. It is convenient and dependable, particularly if you do not know German.

Uber: Uber operates in Frankfurt and offers an alternative to regular taxis. The app is user-friendly and provides a variety of transportation alternatives.

For additional information, go to www.free-now.com.

Walking Tours

Frankfurt is a city best experienced on foot, since many of its attractions are within walking distance of one another. Walking tours provide an excellent opportunity to learn about the city's history, culture, and hidden jewels.

Guided walking tours

Frankfurt City Walks: These guided excursions visit key landmarks such as the Römer, Frankfurt Cathedral, and Goethe House. The expert guides offer unique insights into the city's history and present.

Alternative Walking Tours: For a unique viewpoint, consider taking an alternative walking tour concentrating on street art, local markets, or the city's culinary culture. These trips frequently take you off the usual route, revealing a side of Frankfurt that few tourists witness.

For additional information about guided tours, please visit the Frankfurt Tourism website at www.frankfurt-tourismus.de.

Access for Disabled Travelers

Frankfurt is committed to making itself accessible to all travelers. The city has made substantial efforts to make public transportation, attractions, and public places accessible to individuals with disabilities.

Public Transportation:

Most U-Bahn and S-Bahn stations have elevators and ramps, and the trains are wheelchair-accessible. Buses and trams have low floors and ramps for easy access.

Attractions:

Many of Frankfurt's top attractions, like as museums, theaters, and parks, are wheelchair accessible. For example, the Städel Museum and the Palmengarten include amenities for guests with mobility impairments.

Resources:

The Frankfurt Tourism website provides thorough information on accessibility, including accessible routes and services. Furthermore, the software "Wheelmap" allows you to identify and review accessible locations in the city.

For additional information, see www.frankfurt-tourismus.de/en/Discover-Experience/Barrier-Free-Frankfurt.

Airport Transfers

Traveling to and from Frankfurt Airport is simple owing to a multitude of transit choices.

Public Transportation:

S-Bahn lines S8 and S9 connect Frankfurt Airport to the city center, with trains departing every 15 minutes. The travel to Hauptbahnhof takes around 15 minutes, making it a quick and convenient choice.

Airport shuttle services:

Several shuttle services run between the airport and other sites across Frankfurt. These shuttles may be reserved in advance and provide door-to-door service.

Taxis and ridesharing:

Taxis are easily accessible outside both terminals at Frankfurt Airport. The travel to the city center takes around 20-30 minutes, depending on traffic. Ride-sharing services, such as Uber, are also available.

Car Rental:

If you prefer the freedom of driving, automobile rental desks are available at both Terminals 1 and 2. Hertz, Avis, and Europcar are among the major automobile rental businesses that provide a diverse selection of vehicles.

For additional information about airport transfers, see the Frankfurt Airport website at www.frankfurt-airport.com.

Conclusion

Frankfurt's extensive transit system makes it simple to explore the city and its surrounds. Frankfurt accommodates to all travel inclinations, including the ease of public transportation, the flexibility of bike or driving, and the intimacy of walking tours. Getting about Frankfurt is a breeze, thanks to wheelchair-accessible alternatives and quick airport connections.

Understanding the various modes of transportation and following the supplied recommendations will allow you to travel Frankfurt with ease and confidence. This dynamic city has a lot to offer, and with the correct transportation, you'll be able to make the most of your stay. Enjoy your travels!

CHAPTER 3

ACCOMMODATION IN FRANKFURT

Finding the appropriate location to stay can greatly improve your trip experience, and Frankfurt has a variety of lodging alternatives to suit every budget and desire. During my time in this hectic city, I've had the opportunity to stay in a variety of lodgings, ranging from fancy hotels to comfortable hostels. Here's a step-by-step guide to finding the ideal location to stay in Frankfurt.

Overview of Accommodation Options

Frankfurt's varied selection of lodgings guarantees that any visitor may find an appropriate location to stay. Frankfurt's lodging options range from magnificence to affordability, unique experiences, and all in between. The city is home to luxury hotels with world-class amenities, budget-friendly hotels that do not sacrifice comfort, attractive boutique hotels, convivial hostels, and one-of-a-kind experiences like as serviced flats and Airbnb rentals.

Luxury Hotels

Frankfurt's finest hotels provide an unmatched experience for visitors seeking pleasure and high-quality service. These facilities have attractive decor, excellent service, and a variety of amenities geared to pleasure its customers.

Jumeirah Frankfurt

Jumeirah Frankfurt, located in the center of the city, is well-known for its modern design and opulent facilities. The hotel has large rooms with beautiful city views, a gourmet restaurant, a wellness center, and a swimming pool.

Address: Thurn-und-Taxis-Platz 2, 60313 Frankfurt am Main.

- Site: www.jumeirah.com.

Steigenberger Frankfurter Hof

Steigenberger Frankfurter Hof is one of Frankfurt's most recognizable hotels, combining historical elegance with contemporary grandeur. The hotel has nicely appointed rooms, a Michelin-starred restaurant, and a spa that includes a classic Turkish bath.

- Address: Am Kaiserplatz, 60311 Frankfurt am Main.

- Website address: www.steigenberger.com

Villa Kennedy

Villa Kennedy, housed in a magnificent villa, provides a calm getaway in the middle of Frankfurt. The hotel has elegant rooms, a verdant courtyard, a magnificent spa, and a well regarded Italian restaurant.

- Address: Kennedyallee 70, 60596, Frankfurt am Main.

- Site: www.roccofortehotels.com.

Budget-Friendly Hotels

Traveling on a budget does not imply sacrificing comfort. Frankfurt features a number of affordable hotels that provide clean, pleasant rooms and basic facilities.

MEININGER Hotel, Frankfurt/Main Airport

This hotel, conveniently located near Frankfurt Airport, is ideal for budget-conscious tourists. It has contemporary rooms, a bar, a gaming area, and a guest kitchen.

Address: Bessie-Coleman-Straße 11, 60549 Frankfurt am Main.

- Website: www.meininger-hotels.com.

Hotel Excelsior

Hotel Excelsior, located near Frankfurt Hauptbahnhof, offers pleasant accommodations and a full breakfast buffet. The central position gives it an excellent starting point for exploring the city.

Address: Mannheimer Straße 7-9, 60329 Frankfurt am Main.

- URL: www.hotelexcelsior-frankfurt.de.

ibis Frankfurt Centrum

The ibis Frankfurt Centrum is a solid alternative for budget tourists, offering clean rooms, a 24-hour bar, and a handy location near the Main River.

Address: Speyerer Straße 4, 60327 Frankfurt am Main.

- Site: www.ibis.com.

Boutique Hotels

Frankfurt's boutique hotels provide a more customized and intimate experience, with unique charm and character. These modest venues frequently include unique design elements and personal service.

25 Hours Hotel The Goldman

This contemporary hotel in the Ostend neighborhood offers lively, distinctively furnished rooms inspired by local characters. The hotel also has a popular restaurant and bar.

- Address: Hanauer Landstraße 127, 60314 Frankfurt am Main.

- URL: www.25hours-hotels.com.

The Pure

The Pure, as the name implies, focuses on minimalist, white décor and a tranquil ambiance. This boutique hotel in the Gallus district features contemporary rooms, a zen garden, and a spa center.

- Address: Niddastraße 86, 60329 Frankfurt am Main.

- Website address: www.the-pure.de

Libertine Lindenberg

This boutique hotel combines the conveniences of home with the benefits of a hotel. Located in the bustling Sachsenhausen district, it has colorful design, social areas, and a fully equipped kitchen for guests.

- Address: Frankensteiner Straße 20, 60594 Frankfurt am Main.

- Web address: www.lindenberg.com.

Hostels

Hostels are ideal for solitary travelers, backpackers, or anybody wishing to meet other travelers in a social setting. Frankfurt's hostels provide economical lodging with communal facilities and a welcoming atmosphere.

5 Elements Hostel

Five Elements Hostel, located near the Hauptbahnhof, is well-known for its vibrant environment and social activities. It has dormitory and private rooms, a bar, and a shared kitchen.

- Address: Moselstraße 40, 60329 Frankfurt am Main.

- Website address: www.5elementshostel.de

Frankfurt Hostel

Frankfurt Hostel, located immediately near to the major train station, gives quick access to the city's attractions. The hostel provides complimentary breakfast, a bar, and a variety of activities to help visitors socialize.

- Address: Kaiserstraße 74, 60329 Frankfurt am Main.

- Website address: www.frankfurt-hostel.com

A&O Frankfurt, Galluswarte

A&O Frankfurt Galluswarte, a prominent chain hostel, provides affordable dormitories and individual rooms. It has a rooftop bar with magnificent views of the city.

Address: Mainzer Landstraße 226-230, 60327 Frankfurt am Main.

- Site: www.aohostels.com.

Unique stays (apartments, serviced residences)

Frankfurt has a range of one-of-a-kind accommodations, including serviced apartments and Airbnb rentals. These accommodations provide additional room and freedom, making them suitable for extended visits or those who prefer self-catering.

Adina Apartment Hotel, Frankfurt Neue Oper

This serviced apartment hotel has large studios and apartments that have fully furnished kitchens. It is located near the opera house and has an indoor pool, a fitness facility, and breathtaking views of the city.

- Address: Wilhelm-Leuschner-Straße 6, 60329 Frankfurt am Main.

- Website address: www.adinahotels.com

Capri by Fraser Frankfurt.

Capri by Fraser is located in the Europaviertel neighborhood and provides contemporary apartments with kitchenettes. The hotel also has a gym, a bar, and a restaurant.

- Address: Europa Allee 42, 60327 Frankfurt am Main.

- Website address: www.frasershospitality.com

Airbnb rentals

Airbnb provides a diverse selection of rental alternatives in Frankfurt, including small flats in the city center and attractive houses in calmer suburbs. Staying at an Airbnb allows you to explore the city like a local while yet enjoying the comforts of home.

For additional information, go to www.airbnb.com

Top Recommended Hotels and Resorts

Based on my experiences and suggestions from other tourists, these are some of the best hotels and resorts in Frankfurt:

Roomers Frankfurt

Roomers Frankfurt, a sleek design hotel in the Bahnhofsviertel neighborhood, is well-known for its modern decor, opulent services, and lively nightlife. The hotel has a sophisticated bar, a fine dining restaurant, and a rooftop spa with spectacular views of the city.

- Address: Gutleutstraße 85, 60329 Frankfurt am Main.

- Website address: www.roomers-hotels.com

The Westin Grand Frankfurt

The Westin Grand is located in the center of Frankfurt and provides exquisite rooms, a luxury spa, and a variety of eating options. The hotel's central position offers it an excellent starting point for visiting the city's attractions, retail areas, and cultural sites.

- Address: Konrad-Adenauer-Straße 7, 60313 Frankfurt am Main.

- Website address: www.marriott.com

Innside Frankfurt Eurotheum

This new hotel has rooms with breathtaking panoramic views of Frankfurt's skyline. The hotel, located in the financial area, offers large, contemporary rooms, a sophisticated bar, and convenient access to key business districts.

- Address: Neue Mainzer Straße 66–68, 60311 Frankfurt am Main

- Web address: www.melia.com.

Choosing the Right Accommodation for You

Choosing the proper hotel is determined by your budget, tastes, and the purpose of your vacation. Here are some suggestions to help you decide:

Luxury Seekers:

If you want excellent service, opulent amenities, and a convenient location, try staying at the Jumeirah Frankfurt, Steigenberger Frankfurter Hof, or Villa Kennedy. These hotels provide the best accommodations and are ideal for visitors seeking to indulge in luxury.

Budget travellers:

MEININGER Hotel Frankfurt/Main Airport, Hotel Excelsior, and ibis Frankfurt Centrum provide economical yet decent lodgings. These hotels provide needed facilities and handy locations while remaining affordable.

Boutique enthusiasts:

Travelers looking for unique and personal encounters might go at 25hours Hotel The Goldman, The Pure, or Libertine Lindenberg. These boutique hotels provide customized attention and a distinct style, making your stay unforgettable.

Social Travelers:

If you appreciate meeting other travelers and want a more communal setting, Five Elements Hostel, Frankfurt Hostel, and A&O Frankfurt Galluswarte are great options. These hostels include social events and activities, allowing guests to connect with other visitors.

Long-term stays:

For longer stays or those who like the comforts of home, serviced apartments such as Adina Apartment Hotel Frankfurt Neue Oper, Capri by Fraser Frankfurt, or Airbnb rentals provide additional room and versatility. These lodgings are great for families, business visitors, and individuals want to experience Frankfurt like a native.

Booking Tips & Tricks

Booking your lodging in Frankfurt may be simple if you follow these tips and tactics.

Book in advance

Frankfurt is a popular business and tourist destination, so book your accommodations well in advance, especially during peak seasons and significant events such as trade fairs and festivals.

Compare prices:

Price comparison services such as Booking.com, Expedia, and Hotels.com will help you locate the greatest bargains. These websites frequently provide discounts and special offers, allowing you to save money.

Check reviews:

Read TripAdvisor reviews to obtain a sense of the accommodation's quality and service. Pay attention to recent reviews to verify the information is current.

Consider location:

Select an accommodation that is conveniently positioned near the attractions or regions you intend to visit. Staying near public transportation hubs such as the Hauptbahnhof will help you navigate around the city more easily.

Look for amenities

Consider your preferred facilities, such as free Wi-Fi, breakfast, fitness centers, or parking. Make sure the accommodation has the amenities you want for a comfortable stay.

Flexible booking options:

Choose flexible booking choices that offer free cancellations or changes. This may be useful if your trip plans alter unexpectedly.

Loyalty Programs:

If you often stay at specific hotel chains, think about joining their reward programs. These programs frequently provide rewards like as hotel upgrades, free nights, and unique deals.

Conclusion

Frankfurt has a wide choice of lodging alternatives to accommodate every traveler's needs and interests. Whether you're looking for luxury, affordability, individuality, or a social environment, you'll find the ideal spot to stay in this dynamic city. You may optimize your travel experience by selecting the appropriate hotel based on your budget, tastes, and the purpose of your stay. Remember to book in early, compare costs, and read reviews to guarantee a seamless and pleasurable visit. With the correct accommodations, your stay in Frankfurt will be both pleasant and memorable. Enjoy your travels!

CHAPTER 4

TOP TOURIST ATTRACTIONS

Frankfurt, with its rich history, contemporary skyline, and active culture, has a wide range of activities to appeal to all sorts of tourists. During my visit in this vibrant city, I got the opportunity to discover some of its most recognizable sites and hidden jewels. Here's a full guide to Frankfurt's main tourist sites, each of which provides a unique perspective on the city's eclectic character.

Römer & Römerberg

Römer and Römerberg, located in Frankfurt's old center, are a mesmerizing combination of historical charm and contemporary activity. Römer, the medieval structure that has functioned as Frankfurt's city hall for almost 600 years, is an architectural marvel. Its three-gabled façade is instantly identifiable and popular among photographers. The Kaisersaal (Emperor's Hall) is decorated with pictures of German monarchs, reflecting the grandeur of the Holy Roman Empire.

Römerberg, the square in front of Römer, is similarly lovely. It is surrounded by magnificent half-timbered buildings, each with its own unique tale. Walking across the area, I was taken back in time, picturing the busy market scenes that previously existed here. Today, it remains a bustling focus of activity, particularly during the Frankfurt Christmas Market, one of Germany's oldest and most attractive. The festive ambiance, complete with vendors offering traditional crafts, food, and mulled wine, is delightful.

Address: Römerberg 27, 60311 Frankfurt am Main.

Frankfurt Cathedral

A short stroll from Römerberg will take you to the spectacular Frankfurt Cathedral, also known as St. Bartholomew's Cathedral. This Gothic masterpiece stands out for its red sandstone structure and elaborate architectural elements. The cathedral has played an important role in Frankfurt's history, acting as the coronation church for Holy Roman Emperors for centuries.

Climbing the 328 stairs to the pinnacle of the cathedral tower was one of the highlights of my trip. The panoramic views of Frankfurt's skyline, which combines old buildings and modern skyscrapers, are really beautiful. The cathedral's interior is as spectacular, with towering vaulted ceilings, stunning stained glass windows, and an outstanding main altar.

Address: Domplatz 1, 60311 Frankfurt am Main.

The Städel Museum

For art connoisseurs, the Städel Museum is a must-see. This museum is located on the south bank of the Main River, along the Museum Embankment (Museumsufer), and holds one of Germany's most important art collections. The collection spans over 700 years of European art, with treasures from the Renaissance, Baroque, and Modern eras.

Walking around the galleries, I was captivated by paintings by renowned painters such Rembrandt, Vermeer, Monet, Picasso, and Gerhard Richter. The museum's contemporary wing, with its unique design and natural light, is an excellent setting for modern artworks. The Städel Museum also presents temporary exhibitions, educational activities, and events to make each visit memorable and stimulating.

Address: Schaumainkai 63, 60596, Frankfurt am Main

Website: www.staedelmuseum.de.

Palmengarten

Palmengarten, Frankfurt's botanical garden, provides a tranquil getaway from the city's hustle and bustle. The garden, which spans 22 hectares, has an incredible collection of plants from all around the world. Palmengarten is a nature lover's paradise, with tropical rainforests, dry deserts, rose gardens, and alpine scenery.

The Tropicarium, a collection of greenhouses that replicate various tropical habitats, was one of my favorite sites. Walking inside these glasshouses, I came upon exotic plants, colorful flowers, and even a little waterfall. The garden also organizes seasonal flower exhibitions, concerts, and educational events, making it a popular destination for both pleasure and study.

Address: Siesmayerstraße 61, 60323 Frankfurt am Main.

Website: www.palmengarten.de.

Goethe House

No trip to Frankfurt is complete without paying respect to Johann Wolfgang von Goethe, one of Germany's most famous literary geniuses. Goethe House, the great writer's birthplace, provides an intriguing peek into his early life and the surroundings that created his creativity. The house has been thoroughly renovated to depict Goethe's time there, with authentic furnishings, personal possessions, and family photos.

As I strolled around the rooms, I felt Goethe's presence, particularly in his study, where he wrote some of his early works. The nearby Goethe Museum houses a collection of artworks, manuscripts, and letters that provide further insight into his life and legacy.

Address: Großer Hirschgraben 23-25, 60311 Frankfurt am Main.

Website: www.goethehaus-frankfurt.de.

Main Tower

The Main Tower is a must-see for a genuinely stunning perspective of Frankfurt's skyline. This 56-story skyscraper is one of the few high-rises in Frankfurt with a public observation deck. The elevator trip to the top is an adventure in itself, with views of the city as you rise.

When I arrived at the observation deck, I was treated with panoramic views of Frankfurt and beyond. The cityscape, with its mix of ancient sites and new buildings, is captivating, particularly around sunset. On the 53rd story of the Main Tower, there is a restaurant and bar where you can enjoy great meals while taking in the breathtaking views.

Address: Neue Mainzer Straße 52-58, 60311 Frankfurt am Main.

Website: www.maintower.de.

Senckenberg's Natural History Museum

For anyone interested in natural history and science, the Senckenberg Natural History Museum is a must-see. It is one of Germany's greatest natural history museums, known for its vast collection of fossils, minerals, and taxidermy specimens. The museum's dinosaur bones, notably a gigantic Tyrannosaurus Rex, are a popular attraction for people of all ages.

I was captivated by the museum's eclectic exhibits, which included ancient fossils and meteorites as well as elaborate dioramas of various ecosystems. The museum also has a section dedicated to human evolution, which includes educational displays and interactive exhibits. It's an excellent area to spend a few hours, particularly for families and anyone with a strong interest in nature.

Address: Senckenberganlage 25, 60325 Frankfurt am Main

Website: www.senckenberg.de.

Conclusion

Frankfurt's best tourist sites provide a diverse range of experiences, combining history, art, nature, and modernism. From the historical beauty of Römer and Römerberg to the cutting-edge design of the Main Tower, each location offers a distinct view on the city's eclectic character.

Exploring Frankfurt's cultural treasures, such as the Städel Museum and Goethe House, fosters a greater understanding for the city's creative and literary past. Meanwhile, Palmengarten's natural beauty and the scientific wonders of the Senckenberg Natural History Museum demonstrate the city's dedication to protecting and promoting its natural environment.

As you plan your stay, take the time to immerse yourself in these attractions, each with a unique narrative and experience that adds to Frankfurt's rich mosaic. Frankfurt's finest tourist sites will make a lasting impact, whether you're admiring art, learning about history, or simply taking in the breathtaking vistas. Happy exploring!

CHAPTER 5

EXPLORING THE OLD TOWN

Frankfurt's Old Town, known as the Altstadt, is a compelling neighborhood that seamlessly merges the past with the contemporary. Walking through its cobblestone streets, I felt as if I were moving back in time but still in a bustling, modern metropolis. The Altstadt is full with historical sites, interesting museums, bustling marketplaces, and picturesque riverside walks. Here's a detailed look at what makes Frankfurt's Old Town a must-see trip.

Historical Landmarks

The Römer, Frankfurt's Old Town's city hall, has stood at the center of the Altstadt for almost six centuries and is one of its most recognizable historical structures. Since 1405, this medieval edifice with its characteristic three-gabled exterior has served as the headquarters of Frankfurt's municipal administration. The Römer's interior is as spectacular, with the Kaisersaal (Emperor's Hall) featuring portraits of 52 Holy Roman Emperors. Standing in this hall, I could practically hear the echoes of past events that shaped the city.

Frankfurt Cathedral, also known as St. Bartholomew's Cathedral, is only a short walk from the Römer. This Gothic masterpiece, with its stunning red sandstone building, has played an important role in Frankfurt's history by acting as the coronation cathedral for Holy Roman Emperors. Climbing the cathedral's tower was a highlight of my vacation, since it provided spectacular panoramic views of the metropolis.

St. Nicholas Church, located on Römerberg, is another historical jewel. This little Gothic church, with its attractive exterior and tranquil interior, provides a peaceful respite from the busy plaza. It's a place to sit and ponder while surrounded by millennia of history.

Museums & Galleries

Frankfurt's Old Town is home to several museums and galleries that provide an in-depth look at the city's rich cultural and artistic legacy. One of my favorites is the Historisches Museum Frankfurt, which is located on the banks of the Main River. This museum gives a detailed history of Frankfurt, from its origins as a Roman town to its rise to prominence as a financial center. The interactive exhibitions and elaborate displays bring history to life.

For art aficionados, the Schirn Kunsthalle is a must-see. This contemporary art gallery, near the Römer, has changing exhibitions of modern and contemporary art. The Schirn's unique exhibits and thought-provoking pieces create a lasting impact.

A short walk away is the Museum of Modern Art (MMK), which is situated in a stunning postmodern structure. The MMK has an exceptional collection of modern art, including works by well-known artists including Andy Warhol, Roy Lichtenstein, and Gerhard Richter. The museum's innovative displays and lively atmosphere make it a cultural attraction in Altstadt.

Traditional Markets

Exploring Frankfurt's historic markets is a sensory joy, providing a glimpse into local life and cuisine. The Kleinmarkthalle, a covered market hall on Zeil Shopping Street, is a veritable treasure trove of fresh vegetables, gourmet cuisine, and regional specialties. Walking into the market, I was met by the inviting fragrances of freshly made bread, spices, and flowers. The hectic atmosphere, with sellers shouting out their products and people conversing animatedly, added to the appeal.

One of the market's standouts is the extensive assortment of local sausages, cheeses, and baked items. I couldn't resist sampling a piece of Handkäse, a typical sour milk cheese, and a Frankfurter Würstchen, a sort of sausage specific to the region. The market also offers international delicacies, reflecting Frankfurt's global culture.

During the holiday season, the Frankfurt Christmas Market turns Römerberg and Paulsplatz into a winter paradise. The market's wooden stalls, decked with dazzling lights and Christmas decorations, sell a wide range of crafts, gifts, and seasonal delicacies. Sipping a mug of Glühwein (mulled wine) and snacking on Lebkuchen (gingerbread) while visiting the stalls encapsulates the charm of the Christmas season.

Walking Tours

Walking around Frankfurt's Old Town is one of the greatest ways to discover it. Several guided walking tours are offered, each with a distinct viewpoint on the city's history and culture.

Historic Walking Tour:

This trip visits the Altstadt's significant historical monuments, including the Römer, Frankfurt Cathedral, and St. Nicholas Church. The expert guides tell intriguing anecdotes and insights about Frankfurt's history, bringing it to life.

Culinary Walking Tours:

A gastronomic walking tour is an absolute must-do for foodies. This trip will take you around the Kleinmarkthalle and other local food establishments, where you may sample regional delicacies and learn about Frankfurt's culinary traditions. It's a delightful way to discover the city's thriving culinary industry.

Art and Architecture Tours:

This trip concentrates on the Old Town's artistic and architectural treasures, including visits to the Schirn Kunsthalle and the Museum of Modern Art. The interpreters give detailed commentary on the artworks and architectural styles, making it an interesting experience for art lovers.

Riverside Walks

The Main River is a distinctive feature of Frankfurt, and walking along its banks provides breathtaking vistas as well as a calm getaway from the city's hustle and bustle. The Eiserner Steg, an iron footbridge across the Main River, is an excellent starting place. This pedestrian bridge, ornamented with love locks, offers panoramic views of both the city and the river.

Walking down the Museumsufer (Museum Embankment) on the south side of the Main, I appreciated the picturesque views and cultural attractions that border the river. The embankment houses various museums, including the Städel Museum, the Liebieghaus, and the German Film Museum. The riverbank route is ideal for a leisurely stroll, with seats and green spots to rest and enjoy the views.

During the warmer months, Nizza Park on the northern bank of the Main is a beautiful place to relax. The park's

Mediterranean-style gardens, complete with palm trees and exotic plants, provide a tranquil respite in the center of the city.

Architectural Highlights

Frankfurt's Old Town combines medieval and contemporary architectural elements. One of the most remarkable examples is the Paulskirche (St. Paul's Church), a red sandstone structure with a round, classical shape. This chapel is a symbol of German democracy, as it held the first all-German parliament in 1848. Inside, the basic yet exquisite decor and historical exhibits offer a better appreciation of its significance.

The Haus Wertheim, located on Römerberg, is a unique example of Frankfurt's medieval timber-framed architecture. This lovely home, with its elaborate wooden beams and gabled roof, represents the city's architectural legacy.

Another architectural gem is the Frankfurter Hof, a large hotel with old-world charm. The hotel's elaborate front and lavish interiors evoke the grandeur of a bygone period, making it a symbol of luxury in Altstadt.

Cultural Centres

Frankfurt's Old Town also has various cultural facilities that host a variety of activities and events. The Goethe House and Museum, located near the writer's birthplace, offer an in-depth look into Johann Wolfgang von Goethe's life and work. The house has been renovated to depict the time Goethe resided there, including genuine furniture and personal belongings.

The Frankfurt Opera, located near Willy-Brandt-Platz, is one of Germany's most prominent opera theaters. Attending a performance here is a cultural highlight, since it features world-class opera, ballet, and classical concerts.

The English Theatre Frankfurt, Europe's biggest English-speaking theatre, presents a diversified schedule of plays and musicals. The theatre, located near Kaiserstraße, is a cultural jewel in the Altstadt because to its compact setting and high-quality performances.

Conclusion

Exploring Frankfurt's Old Town is like traveling through time, with history, culture, and current life all intertwined. The Altstadt provides a variety of experiences, from the medieval beauty of the Römer and the majesty of Frankfurt Cathedral to modern art at the Schirn Kunsthalle and colorful markets.

Walking around the Old Town, I was attracted by the architectural variety, the vibrant energy of the markets, and the tranquil serenity of the riverfront walkways. The cultural centers and museums offered in-depth insights into Frankfurt's rich legacy and artistic achievements.

Frankfurt's Old Town provides something for everyone, whether you enjoy history, art, gastronomy, or are simply interested about travel. Take the time to wander its streets, find its hidden treasures, and immerse yourself in the tales that make this section of the city unique. Happy exploring!

CHAPTER 6

MODERN FRANKFURT

Frankfurt is a city of contrasts, where history and innovation coexist harmoniously. During my time in Frankfurt, I was captivated by its energetic modernism, which contrasted with its historical appeal. From the towering buildings of the financial sector to the bustling commercial districts, cutting-edge art, and elegant urban parks, contemporary Frankfurt provides a plethora of experiences. Here's a comprehensive guide to discovering the city's modern side.

Financial Districts and Skyscrapers

Frankfurt's financial district, sometimes known as "Mainhattan" because to its striking skyline, is the throbbing center of Germany's financial industry. Walking through this neighborhood made me feel like I was in a futuristic metropolis, with dazzling buildings reaching for the sky.

Sir Norman Foster built the Commerzbank Tower, Frankfurt's tallest structure. Its environmentally friendly design includes natural lighting and ventilation, establishing a standard for sustainable building. Nearby, the Main Tower has an observation deck with panoramic views of the city. Watching the sunset from the top of the Main Tower, with the city lights flashing below, was a breathtaking experience.

Another recognizable structure is the Eurotower, which houses the European Central Bank. The large blue euro sign on front of the building is a famous picture spot. The Frankfurt Stock Exchange, one of the major trading centers in the world, is also located in the financial sector. Although the trading floor is not accessible to the public, guided tours provide insight into the workings of global finance.

Address: Financial District, 60311 Frankfurt am Main.

Shopping in Zeil.

Zeil, Frankfurt's greatest retail street, is a shoppers' paradise and a busy center of activity. Zeil runs from Hauptwache to Konstablerwache and has a mix of high-end boutiques, department stores, and worldwide chains. The pedestrianized street is ideal for a leisurely shopping experience, with something for everyone.

MyZeil, an architectural wonder with a beautiful glass façade and sweeping interior design, is one of my favorite Zeil destinations. The mall has a diverse selection of businesses, from fashion to electronics, as well as several food options. The panoramic elevators and the longest indoor escalator in Europe enhance the shopping experience.

For those looking for premium labels, Goethestraße, a short walk from Zeil, is the place to go. This exquisite street is home to famous retailers including Louis Vuitton, Prada, and Tiffany & Co. Window shopping here is like walking through an open-air display of fine fashion.

On Saturdays, the Konstablerwache Farmers Market is a must-stop. The market sells fresh fruit, artisanal cheeses, and home-made delights. I enjoyed perusing the vendors, trying local delights, and taking in the colorful ambiance.

Address: Zeil, 60313 Frankfurt am Main.

Contemporary Art and Architecture

Frankfurt's dedication to modern art and architecture is reflected in its thriving cultural scene and creative structures. The Museum of Modern Art (MMK), situated in a remarkable modernist structure, is a key component of the city's contemporary art scene. The MMK's collection contains pieces by Andy Warhol, Roy Lichtenstein, and Gerhard Richter, among others. The museum's vibrant displays and interactive installations are a must-see for art enthusiasts.

Another hidden treasure is the Schirn Kunsthalle, which is located close the Römer. This modern art gallery has rotating shows that explore a variety of subjects and media. The Schirn's unique exhibits and thought-provoking pieces create a lasting impact.

Frankfurt's architectural creativity extends beyond its museums. The Westhafen Tower, with its cylindrical form and glass façade, is a prime example of contemporary design. The tower's honeycomb-like construction is both eye-catching and energy-efficient. Nearby, the Europaviertel neighborhood shows cutting-edge urban development, with elegant residential and commercial structures, public art pieces, and green spaces.

Address: The Museum of Modern Art (MMK), Domstraße 10, 60311 Frankfurt am Main

Website address: www.mmk-frankfurt.de.

Address: Schirn Kunsthalle, Römerberg, 60311, Frankfurt am Main

Website: www.schirn.de.

Modern Parks and Recreation Areas

Frankfurt's new parks and recreation facilities provide a welcome respite from the city's hectic pace. One of my favorite places is Nizza Park, which is located on the northern bank of the Main River. This Mediterranean-style park has palm palms, exotic flora, and a peaceful ambiance. Walking through Nizza Park seemed more like a beach getaway than the midst of a busy metropolis.

The Europagarten in the Europaviertel neighborhood is another contemporary green space worth seeing. This enormous urban park features expansive lawns, playgrounds, and walking routes. It's ideal for picnics, running, or just resting with a book.

For sports fans, the Commerzbank-Arena and its surroundings provide excellent leisure opportunities. Eintracht Frankfurt's stadium is surrounded by beautiful vegetation and routes suitable for cycling and jogging. The nearby Waldstadion Park has other amenities, such as a swimming pool and tennis courts.

Address: Nizza Park, Untermainkai, 60329 Frankfurt am Main.

Address: Europagarten, Europa Allee, 60327 Frankfurt am Main

High-Tech and Innovation Centres

Frankfurt is more than simply a financial hub; it is also a center for innovation and technology. The city is home to numerous high-tech and innovation centers that drive forward progress in a variety of disciplines.

The Frankfurt Innovation Center for Biotechnology (FIZ) is a major hub for biotechnology research and development. FIZ, located in the Höchst Industrial Park, brings together startups, research institutes, and established enterprises to promote collaboration and innovation in the life sciences industry. When I visited the FIZ, I was struck by the cutting-edge laboratories and the entrepreneurial spirit that pervades the institution.

In terms of information technology, the TechQuartier is Frankfurt's primary startup cluster. TechQuartier, located in the center of the financial sector, offers coworking spaces, mentorship programs, and networking opportunities for technology entrepreneurs. The active community and dynamic climate make it an appealing destination for everyone interested in the technology business.

The House of Finance at Goethe University is another important actor in Frankfurt's innovation scene. This multidisciplinary research center specializes on finance, monetary economics, and corporate governance. The center's seminars and conferences draw researchers and professionals from all over the world, adding to Frankfurt's status as a thought leader in financial research.

Address: Frankfurt Innovation Centre for Biotechnology (FIZ), G8363, 65926 Frankfurt am Main.

Website: www.fiz-biotech.de.

Address: Techquartier, Platz der Einheit 2, 60327 Frankfurt am Main.

Website address: www.techquartier.com.

Urban Development Projects

Frankfurt's skyline is constantly changing, due to ambitious urban development initiatives that are redefining the city's landscape. One of the most prominent initiatives is the Europaviertel area, a huge development that has turned a derelict train yard into a thriving mixed-use community.

Europaviertel includes a variety of residential, commercial, and recreational facilities, such as the Skyline Plaza retail complex, the Kap Europa convention center, and other contemporary business buildings. The district's open spaces, such as Europagarten, provide inhabitants and tourists several options for outdoor recreation.

Another notable development is Frankfurt Gateway Gardens, an innovative commercial neighborhood near Frankfurt Airport. This environmentally friendly initiative aspires to create a sustainable urban environment with energy-efficient buildings, green roofs, and expansive parklands. The area was created to attract foreign enterprises and promote a global business community.

The Osthafen sector, located on the eastern banks of the Main River, is being transformed into a vibrant waterfront region. The redevelopment plans call for contemporary residential complexes, cultural events, and recreational amenities. The idea is to create a vibrant urban place that blends work, living, and leisure in a scenic location.

Address: Europaviertel, Europa Allee, 60327 Frankfurt am Main.

Address: Frankfurt Gateway Gardens, Amelia-Mary-Earhart-Straße, 60549 Frankfurt am Main.

Conclusion

Modern Frankfurt is a city of creativity and sophistication, with cutting-edge architecture, high-tech institutions, and thriving cultural scenes coexisting peacefully. From the dazzling towers of the financial sector to the busy shopping strip of Zeil, the city is alive with energy and excitement.

Exploring modern art at the Museum of Modern Art, strolling through the elegant Europagarten, and visiting innovation hubs such as TechQuartier all provide insight into Frankfurt's forward-thinking ethos. The city's major urban development initiatives, like Europaviertel and Frankfurt Gateway Gardens, demonstrate its commitment to long-term growth and urban rehabilitation.

Whether you're admiring the architectural glories of Manhattan, indulging in retail therapy on Zeil, or unwinding in a modern park, Frankfurt's contemporary side has something for every tourist. Accept the city's dynamic vitality and explore the diverse activities that make contemporary Frankfurt an interesting visit. Happy exploring!

CHAPTER 7

CULTURAL EXPERIENCES

Frankfurt, Germany, is a city rich in culture and vivid experiences that embody both its historical origins and present energy. During my stay in this wonderful city, I had the opportunity to immerse myself in its rich cultural attractions. From boisterous festivals to quiet theatrical performances, every encounter left an indelible imprint. Allow me to guide you through some of the greatest cultural activities Frankfurt has to offer.

Traditional Festivities and Events

Frankfurt's calendar is jam-packed with festivals and events that honor its rich history and varied citizenry. One of the most major yearly events is the Frankfurt Book Fair (Frankfurter Buchmesse), the world's biggest book fair.

Every October, publishers, authors, and literary fans from around the world visit the city. The fair is a literary carnival, complete with book signings, readings, and debates. I was particularly drawn to the bright environment and the opportunity to meet writers and discover new books.

Another attraction is the Frankfurt Christmas Market, which transforms Römerberg and Paulsplatz into a holiday paradise. The market, with its wooden stalls, shimmering lights, and perfume of Glühwein (mulled wine), embodies the charm of the Christmas season. Strolling through the market, sipping hot chocolate, and admiring homemade products was a great opportunity to learn about German Christmas traditions.

In the summer, the Museum Embankment Festival (Museumsuferfest) is a must-see. This event highlights Frankfurt's rich museum culture with open-air concerts, art displays, and performances along the Main River. The bustling atmosphere, with food booths and craft merchants line the riverbank, provides an ideal combination of art and entertainment.

Frankfurt Book Fair website: www.buchmesse.de.

Frankfurt Christmas Market website: www.frankfurt-tourismus.de.

Museum Embankment Festival (www.museumsuferfest.de)

Local Music and Dance

Frankfurt's music culture is diversified, including classical performances and contemporary music festivals. The Alte Oper (Old Opera House) is a magnificent theater that presents a wide range of acts, including classical music, opera, and ballet. Attending a concert here is a wonderful experience due to the grandeur of the venue and the quality of the performers. One of my favorite evenings in Frankfurt was spent listening to Beethoven's symphony in this amazing venue.

For fans of modern music, the Jazzkeller is a famed venue. Jazzkeller, located in a basement in the city center, has served as a gathering place for jazz fans since the 1950s. The small environment, as well as the selection of local and international musicians, provide for an ideal setting for live jazz. I spent several hours here, captivated by the passionate performances.

Dance enthusiasts should not miss Ballett Frankfurt, the city's top ballet group. Their performances at the Oper Frankfurt highlight the beauty and accuracy of ballet. In addition, the Tanzhaus West provides a more modern dance environment, with events and seminars that explore many dance forms and cultures.

Alte Oper (www.alteoper.de)

Jazzkeller (www.jazzkeller.com)

Oper Frankfurt (www.oper-frankfurt.de)

Art Gallery and Studio

Frankfurt's art scene is both diversified and accessible, with various galleries and studios exhibiting a diverse spectrum of artistic styles. The Städel Museum is an important part of Frankfurt's cultural environment, with a vast collection of European art from the Middle Ages to the present. Walking through its galleries, I was enthralled by works by Rembrandt, Monet, and Picasso.

For contemporary art fans, the Museum of Modern Art (MMK) is a must-see. The museum's collection contains works by prominent contemporary artists and provides a stimulating examination of modern art. The museum's creative architecture is worthy of admiration.

Smaller, independent galleries, such as the Galerie Moritz and Galerie Anita Beckers, provide a more personal experience by displaying rising artists and cutting-edge works. These galleries are ideal for discovering emerging artists and one-of-a-kind works.

Furthermore, the Frankfurt Art Walk is a great opportunity to discover the city's art culture. This self-guided tour will take you through many galleries, studios, and public art projects. It's a great way to spend the afternoon, immersed in Frankfurt's creative spirit.

Städel Museum (www.staedelmuseum.de)

Museum of Modern Art (MMK) website: www.mmk-frankfurt.de

Frankfurt Art Walk: http://www.frankfurt-tourismus.de

Theatre and Performing Arts

Theater and performing arts play an important role in Frankfurt's cultural life. The Schauspiel Frankfurt is one of Germany's top theaters, known for its creative shows and outstanding performances. The theater's repertory consists of a mix of classic and current pieces, many with a distinct and modern spin. Attending a play at Schauspiel Frankfurt was always a stimulating and enlightening experience.

For English-speaking guests, the English Theatre Frankfurt presents a variety of plays and musicals in English. It is continental Europe's largest English-speaking theater, with productions noted for their outstanding quality and captivating storyline. I saw an excellent version of "The Rocky Horror Show" here, replete with audience involvement and entertainment.

The Frankfurt Opera is another hidden treasure, offering world-class opera and ballet performances. The magnificent location and great ability of the artists make it a must-see for every cultural fan. One of the most memorable nights I spent in Frankfurt was attending a stunning staging of "La Traviata."

Schauspiel Frankfurt (www.schauspielfrankfurt.de)

English Theatre Frankfurt (www.english-theatre.de)

Frankfurt Opera website: www.oper-frankfurt.de

Culinary Experiences and Classes

Frankfurt's culinary scene offers a fascinating blend of traditional German cuisine and cosmopolitan influences. Taking a cooking class is an excellent opportunity to immerse yourself in the city's culinary culture. Cooking Time provides lessons where you can learn how to create classic German foods such as Sauerbraten (pot roast) and Apfelwein (apple wine). These sessions are a fun and delightful journey since they provide hands-on experience and allow you to taste your creations.

Zum Gemalten Haus in Sachsenhausen is a great spot to try local dishes like Handkäse mit Musik (a regional cheese dish) and Grüne Soße (green sauce). The rustic environment and substantial dishes offer a true flavor of Frankfurt's culinary history.

If you like foreign food, Fressgass (formally known as Große Bockenheimer Straße) is a bustling street lined with restaurants and cafés serving a variety of cuisines. From Italian trattorias to sushi restaurants, there's something for everyone to enjoy.

The Main Tower Restaurant & Lounge provides a one-of-a-kind dining experience by serving exceptional cuisine while overlooking the city. Dining here at sunset, with the skyline lit up below, was a wonderful experience.

Cooking Time (www.cooking-time.de)

Zum Gemalten Haus website: www.zumgemaltenhaus.de.

Main Tower Restaurant & Lounge: http://www.maintower-restaurant.de

Cultural Tours and Workshops

A cultural tour or class might help you better grasp Frankfurt's rich background. The Frankfurt City Tour provides a variety of specialized tours, including historical walks, architectural tours, and gastronomic excursions. These excursions are given by skilled guides who provide interesting facts and tales about the city.

For a hands-on cultural experience, the Frankfurt School of Crafts provides classes in traditional crafts like as ceramics, woodworking, and printing. Participating in a pottery class was a pleasure for me since I got to produce my own piece of Frankfurt-inspired art.

The Jewish Museum Frankfurt offers guided excursions of the history and culture of Frankfurt's Jewish community. The museum's displays and educational activities provide visitors a thorough and moving grasp of the community's contributions and experiences.

Frankfurt City Tour (www.frankfurt-tourismus.de)

Frankfurt School of Crafts (www.handwerk-schule.de)

Jewish Museum, Frankfurt: www.juedischesmuseum.de

Libraries & Literature

Frankfurt has a rich literary legacy, as it was the birthplace of Johann Wolfgang von Goethe, one of Germany's best writers. The Goethe House and Museum is a must-see for literary fans. The house where Goethe was born and spent his childhood has been lovingly renovated to suit the period's décor. The museum next door houses manuscripts, letters, and pictures that give insight into Goethe's life and work.

The German National Library (Deutsche Nationalbibliothek) in Frankfurt is another literary gem. This massive library holds millions of volumes, manuscripts, and journals, making it an ideal destination for scholars and book enthusiasts. The library's galleries and reading spaces provide a calm setting for exploring German literature and history.

The Frankfurt Book Fair offers a more contemporary literary experience. As the world's largest book expo, it attracts writers, publishers, and literary aficionados from all over the world. The fair includes book signings, readings, and debates, creating a dynamic and interesting atmosphere for book enthusiasts.

Frankfurt's public libraries (Stadtbücherei Frankfurt) provide a multitude of materials and activities. The central library at the Hauptwache conducts public author readings, seminars, and cultural activities. Spending a day here, reading the huge collection and attending a literary program, was both pleasant and enriching.

Goethe House and Museum: http://www.goethehaus-frankfurt.de

German National Library website: www.dnb.de.

Frankfurt Public Libraries: http://stadtbuecherei.frankfurt.de

Conclusion

Frankfurt's cultural landscape is as dynamic and diversified as the city itself. Traditional festivals and world-class music venues, as well as cutting-edge art galleries and small theater performances, will enthrall every visitor. These cultural events improved my time in Frankfurt, each providing a distinct insight into the city's essence.

Whether you're attending a festival, studying art, going on a gastronomic journey, or delving into the city's literary past, Frankfurt's cultural attractions are guaranteed to leave an impact. Take the time to immerse yourself in these experiences, and you will uncover the rich tapestry that makes Frankfurt such an intriguing and vibrant location. Happy exploring!

CHAPTER 8

DAYTRIPS FROM FRANKFURT

Frankfurt is an excellent location for seeing some of Germany's most lovely and historically significant attractions. Each day excursion provides a distinct combination of culture, history, and natural beauty. After spending a lot of time traveling from Frankfurt, I've put up a thorough guide to some of the greatest day trips you can take, each of which offers a unique experience. Allow me to take you on a tour through these beautiful locales.

Heidelberg

Heidelberg is one of Germany's most charming cities, known for its attractive old town, imposing castle, and lively university scene. Heidelberg, located just a short train ride from Frankfurt, is an ideal day trip destination.

My favorite part of my trip to Heidelberg was the Heidelberg Castle, which sits on a hill overlooking the city and the Neckar River. The castle, with its Gothic and Renaissance design, provides breathtaking vistas and a rich history. Walking around the castle ruins and gardens, I felt as if I had traveled back in time. Don't miss the Heidelberg Tun, a massive wine barrel that holds over 220,000 liters of wine.

Another popular attraction in Heidelberg is the Philosophenweg (Philosopher's Walk). This lovely walking trail provides a panoramic view of the ancient town and castle. As I walked along the road, I saw why poets and philosophers found inspiration here.

Heidelberg's old town is a lovely tangle of cobblestone lanes, antique houses, and cozy cafés. The Marktplatz, with its Baroque architecture and vibrant ambiance, is an excellent location to begin. Visit the Church of the Holy Spirit and the Heidelberg University Library, both of which have rich histories.

Address: Heidelberg Castle, Schlosshof 1, 69117 Heidelberg.

Website: www.schloss-heidelberg.de.

Mainz

Rhineland-Palatinate's capital, Mainz, is well-known for its rich history, dynamic culture, and link to Johannes Gutenberg, the creator of the movable-type printing machine. Mainz, a 30-minute rail trip from Frankfurt, combines ancient monuments with modern flair.

Anyone interested in printing and book history should pay a visit to the Gutenberg Museum. The museum displays authentic Gutenberg Bibles and illustrates the printing process. As a book enthusiast, witnessing these historical items up close was an exciting experience.

Mainz's cathedral (Mainzer Dom) is another feature. This remarkable Romanesque structure, with its red sandstone front and elaborate interior, has been an integral part of Mainz for over a millennium. The cathedral's crypts and cloisters are especially interesting to explore.

St. Stephan's Church, known for its spectacular blue stained glass windows built by Marc Chagall, is a peaceful and lovely location to visit. The windows emit a stunning blue light throughout the chapel, providing a serene and reflecting ambiance.

Mainz's old town, with its half-timbered homes and small lanes, is ideal for a relaxing stroll. The Augustinerstrasse is a bustling boulevard lined with stores, cafés, and historic houses. A glass of local Riesling wine in a nice wine bar was the ideal way to round out my day in Mainz.

Address: Gutenberg Museum, Liebfrauenplatz 5, 55116 Mainz.

Website: www.gutenberg-museum.de.

Wiesbaden

Wiesbaden, Hesse's capital, is a magnificent spa town with fine architecture, thermal spas, and a thriving cultural scene. Wiesbaden, just a short rail ride from Frankfurt, provides a calm and enriching day excursion.

One of Wiesbaden's biggest attractions is the Kurhaus, a beautiful neoclassical structure that contains a casino and a performance venue. The Kurhaus, surrounded by beautiful gardens and fountains, represents Wiesbaden's grandeur. I took a leisurely walk through the Kurpark, admiring the lovely landscaping and quiet environment.

The Wilhelmstrasse, often known as the "Rue," is Wiesbaden's most renowned street. It's a wonderful destination to visit, with its exquisite shops, cafés, and old buildings. The Hessisches Staatstheater on Wilhelmstrasse is a spectacular arena that offers a wide range of acts, including opera, ballet, and theater.

For a genuinely soothing experience, go to one of Wiesbaden's famed thermal spas. The Kaiser-Friedrich-Therme is a stunning Art Nouveau bathhouse that has a variety of thermal pools, saunas, and health services. Soaking in the warm waters and getting a massage was an excellent way to relax.

Wiesbaden's Neroberg Hill provides breathtaking views of the city and surrounding region. To get to the summit, take the old Nerobergbahn funicular railway. The hill is home to the stunning Greek Chapel and the Neroberg Temple, both of which are worth a visit.

Address: Kurhaus, Kurhausplatz 1, 65189 Wiesbaden.

Website: www.wiesbaden.de.

The Rhine Valley

The Rhine Valley, a UNESCO World Heritage site, is known for its breathtaking scenery, medieval castles, and attractive villages. A day excursion from Frankfurt to the Rhine Valley takes you through one of Germany's most gorgeous places.

A river cruise is an excellent way to discover the Rhine Valley. Cruises leave from cities like as Rüdesheim and Bingen, providing beautiful views of the castles and vineyards that border the rivers. As I cruised down the Rhine, I was enthralled by the fairy-tale landscape and feeling of timeless beauty.

Rüdesheim is a lovely village that acts as a gateway to the Rhine Valley. The Drosselgasse, a short lane surrounded with half-timbered houses, is brimming with bustling wine bars and businesses. A visit to Siegfried's Mechanical Music Cabinet, a museum of automated musical instruments, was both interesting and enjoyable.

The Lorelei Rock, a steep rock on the Rhine's banks, is steeped in folklore and provides breathtaking views of the river. The rock is related with the Lorelei mythology, which tells of a siren who used her alluring song to lure sailors to their deaths.

Bacharach, another Rhine Valley treasure, is a lovely town with ancient architecture and a fascinating history. The town's half-timbered buildings and cobblestone streets lend a quaint and picturesque air. Exploring the ruins of Stahleck Castle, positioned high above the town, offers both adventure and spectacular vistas.

Website address: www.rhein-tourismus.de.

Darmstadt

Darmstadt, often known as the "City of Science," is a thriving city with a rich cultural legacy and a strong focus on innovation and education. Darmstadt, located just a 20-minute rail ride from Frankfurt, provides a unique combination of history, art, and science.

Darmstadt's most notable attraction is the Mathildenhöhe, an artists' community created in 1899. The colony is home to the Wedding Tower, constructed by Joseph Maria Olbrich, as well as other Art Nouveau structures and sculptures. Walking through Mathildenhöhe, I was captivated by the beauty and ingenuity of the buildings and gardens.

The Hessisches Landesmuseum is a must-see for art and history buffs. The museum's broad collection ranges from prehistoric items to current art. I really liked the natural history exhibitions and the huge collection of Art Nouveau artifacts.

For people interested in science and technology, the European Space Operations Centre (ESOC) provides guided tours of space missions and satellite operations. The excursions are instructive and exciting, emphasizing Darmstadt's significance in space exploration.

Darmstadt's city center has full with attractive streets and squares, notably the largest plaza, Luisenplatz. The area is flanked by ancient buildings and bustling eateries, making it an ideal spot to unwind and people-watch.

Address: Mathildenhöhe, Olbrichweg 15, 64287 Darmstadt.

Website address: www.mathildenhoehe.eu.

Taunus Mountains

The Taunus Mountains, just north of Frankfurt, provide a stunning natural getaway with undulating hills, lush woods, and lovely towns. The location is ideal for hiking, motorcycling, and enjoying the great outdoors.

One of the Taunus Mountains' attractions is the Großer Feldberg, the range's tallest mountain. The top provides panoramic views of the surrounding area and is a popular spot for hiking and bicycling. The observation tower at the summit offers even more amazing views.

Bad Homburg, at the foot of the Taunus Mountains, is well-known for its thermal baths and spa culture. The Kurpark in Bad Homburg is a wonderfully designed park with fountains, sculptures, and walkways. The Kur-Royal Day

Spa provided a revitalizing experience with its thermal bath and health treatments.

The Saalburg Roman Fort, a recreated Roman fort and museum, provides an intriguing look at the history of the Roman Empire in the Taurus area. The fort's displays and guided tours give insight into Roman soldiers' everyday lives as well as the area's history.

Königstein, with its historic castle and lovely old town, is another hidden treasure of the Taunus Mountains. Exploring the remains of Königstein Castle and walking through the town's small alleyways was a lovely experience.

Website address: www.taunus.info.

Aschaffenburg

Aschaffenburg, located on the banks of the Main River, is a lovely town recognized for its historical sites and gorgeous surroundings. Aschaffenburg, located just a short train trip from Frankfurt, provides a lovely combination of culture, history, and natural beauty.

The Johannisburg Castle, a splendid Renaissance castle, is the focal point of Aschaffenburg. The castle has various museums, including the Schlossmuseum, which displays collections of art, furniture, and historical items. Walking around the castle's great halls and admiring its lovely gardens was a highlight of my trip.

The Pompejanum, a Roman villa model, is another one-of-a-kind attraction in Aschaffenburg. The Pompejanum, built in the nineteenth century and inspired by Pompeii's buildings, boasts exquisite mosaics, paintings, and classical architecture. The villa's placement on a hill overlooking the Main River adds to its appeal.

Aschaffenburg's old town, with its tiny lanes and half-timbered homes, is ideal for a stroll. The Stiftsplatz, the main plaza, is flanked by ancient buildings and bustling eateries. Drinking coffee on the plaza and watching the world go by was a peaceful way to spend the day.

The Park Schönbusch, one of Germany's oldest English landscape gardens, is a lovely spot to relax and enjoy the outdoors. The park has lakes, meadows, walking pathways, and a lovely chateau and pavilion. A leisurely stroll around the park's lovely surroundings was an ideal way to finish my day in Aschaffenburg.

Address: Johannisburg Castle, Schlossplatz 4, 63739 Aschaffenburg.

Website: www.schloesser.bayern.de.

Conclusion

Frankfurt's strategic position gives it an excellent base for seeing some of Germany's most beautiful and historically significant places. Each day tour offers a distinct combination of culture, history, and natural beauty, allowing for a better knowledge of the region's complex legacy.

Whether you're strolling through the charming alleys of Heidelberg, discovering the cultural riches of Mainz, resting in Wiesbaden's hot springs, or traveling down the gorgeous Rhine Valley, each site guarantees a unique experience. The Taunus Mountains give a natural respite with hiking and bike paths, while Darmstadt's mix of art and science creates an exciting cultural adventure. Aschaffenburg's historical sites and attractive environment contribute to the allure of visiting the area.

These day trips from Frankfurt not only enrich your travel experience, but also provide you with lasting memories of Germany's rich cultural tapestry. Take the time to visit these great spots and you will discover the beauty and diversity that make this region unique. Happy exploring!

CHAPTER 9

FAMILY-FRIENDLY ACTIVITIES

Frankfurt is an excellent family destination, with a variety of activities suitable for both children and adults. Frankfurt has something for everyone, whether you're visiting zoos and animal parks, exploring interactive museums, or enjoying the city's many parks and playgrounds. During my stay in Frankfurt, I discovered several family-friendly sites and activities that made our trip extremely unforgettable. Here is a comprehensive list to the top family-friendly activities in Frankfurt.

Zoos and Animal Parks

One of the pleasures of our family trip to Frankfurt was seeing the Frankfurt Zoo. This zoo, located in the middle of the city, has around 4,500 species from all over the world.

The zoo's layout is both child-friendly and informative, with themed areas like as the Grzimek habitat, which features nocturnal species, and the Borgori Forest, a large ape habitat.

My children thoroughly enjoyed the zoo's regular feedings and informative speeches. They were very interested about the penguin feeding and elephant bath time. The petting zoo section, where children could interact with goats and lambs, was extremely popular. The Frankfurt Zoo provides an excellent chance for youngsters to learn about nature and conservation in a pleasant and interactive setting.

Another fantastic site for animal enthusiasts is the Opel Zoo, which is located in Kronberg, just outside Frankfurt. This zoo provides a more open and natural environment, with huge cages that resemble the animals' native habitats. My family relished the safari-like experience of roaming amid zebras, giraffes, and antelopes. The playgrounds, picnic spots, and educational activities make it an excellent choice for a family day.

Frankfurt Zoo address: Alfred-Brehm-Platz 16, 60316 Frankfurt am Main.

Website: www.zoo-frankfurt.de.

Opel Zoo, Königsteiner Straße 35, 61476 Kronberg am Taunus.

Website address: www.opel-zoo.de.

Amusement and Theme Parks

Taunus Wunderland is the ideal place to spend an exciting day. Located in the Taunus Mountains, this family-friendly amusement park has rides and activities for all ages. Everyone may enjoy roller coasters and water rides, as well as peaceful carousels and adventure playgrounds. My children enjoyed the pirate-themed section and the fairy tale woodland, which allowed them to explore and play in themed settings.

Another excellent alternative is Holiday Park in Haßloch, which is little further from Frankfurt but well worth the drive. The park has thrilling rides like the Expedition GeForce roller coaster as well as family-friendly attractions like Majaland, which is based on the popular children's mascot Maya the Bee. The park's live entertainment and interactive activities add to the excitement, making it an excellent choice for a family excursion.

For smaller children, Lochmühle Amusement Park in Wehrheim provides a more relaxing and nature-focused experience. The park blends classic fairground rides with farm-themed activities including tractor rides and animal petting areas. My family liked the variety of activities, including riding the miniature train and feeding the farm animals.

Taunus Wunderland, Haus zur Schanze 1, 65388 Schlangenbad.

Website address: www.taunuswunderland.de.

Holiday Park: Holiday-Park-Straße 1–5, 67454 Haßloch

Website: www.holidaypark.de.

Lochmühle Amusement Park address: Lochmühle 1, 61273 Wehrheim.

Website address: www.freizeitpark-lochmuehle.de.

Interactive Museums

Frankfurt is home to various interactive museums that are ideal for families. The Experiminta Science Center is a hands-on museum where kids can discover the marvels of science and technology via interactive displays. The museum's demonstrations and activities encompass subjects such as physics, mathematics, and biology, making learning enjoyable and interesting. My children spent hours at the various stations, creating constructions, playing with water flow, and learning about magnets.

The Senckenberg Natural History Museum is another must-see. The museum, which is well-known for its enormous collection of dinosaur skeletons, takes visitors on a thrilling trip through Earth's past. My children were intrigued by the museum's life-sized dinosaur replicas and interactive displays, and the educational sessions offered deeper insights into natural history.

The Children's Museum Frankfurt is geared at younger visitors, with a range of exhibits and programs that promote creativity and discovery. The museum's interactive displays include subjects such as history, culture, and the environment, making for an enjoyable and instructive experience for children. My family thoroughly enjoyed the hands-on workshops, in which youngsters could paint, craft, and construct.

Experiminta Science Center, Hamburger Allee 22-24, 60486 Frankfurt am Main.

Website: www.experiminta.de.

Senckenberg Natural History Museum (Senckenberganlage 25, 60325 Frankfurt am Main)

Website: www.senckenberg.de.

Children's Museum Frankfurt: An der Hauptwache 15, 60313 Frankfurt am Main.

Website address: www.kindermuseum.frankfurt.de.

Parks and Playgrounds

Frankfurt has several parks and playgrounds where families may enjoy outdoor activities and relax. The Palmengarten is one of the city's most popular green areas, with themed gardens, greenhouses, and a huge playground. The garden's tropical and desert cottages, packed with exotic flora, offered a lovely retreat into nature. My children enjoyed the playground and the tiny lake, where we could hire pedal boats.

Grüneburgpark is another popular family destination, with expansive lawns, shaded walks, and a huge playground. The park's calm ambiance makes it ideal for picnics, games, and just resting. We had fun flying kites and enjoying a family lunch beneath the trees.

Nidda Park, with its expansive playground constructed like a little city, offers a one-of-a-kind experience. The park features a variety of play structures, such as climbing frames, slides, and swings, as well as a water play area that is ideal for hot summer days. The park's vast walking and bike routes, along with its stunning natural landscape, make it an ideal destination for outdoor activities.

Palmengarten, Siesmayerstraße 61, 60323 Frankfurt am Main.

Website: www.palmengarten.de.

Grüneburg Park: August-Siebert-Straße, 60323 Frankfurt am Main.

Website address: www.frankfurt.de.

Nidda Park, Am Ginnheimer Wäldchen, 60431 Frankfurt am Main.

Website address: www.frankfurt.de.

Family-friendly Restaurants

It might be difficult to find a restaurant that serves both adults and children, but Frankfurt has lots of family-friendly dining alternatives. Frankfurter Botschaft, a waterfront restaurant with a calm environment and a menu featuring both local and foreign cuisine, was one of our favorites. The restaurant's outside patio, which overlooks the Main River, was ideal for the kids to play as we had a relaxing supper.

Café Extrablatt in the city center is another excellent choice for families. The café serves breakfast, lunch, and supper, with lots of kid-friendly options. The relaxed atmosphere and nice personnel made it a fun eating experience for the entire family.

Paulaner am Dom is a great place to sample traditional German food. The restaurant's robust cuisine, such as schnitzel and sausages, were popular with both children and adults. The pleasant decor and children's menu make it an inviting spot for families.

If you prefer a more informal eating experience, the Frankfurter Markthalle has a number of food stalls and merchants serving anything from sandwiches to sushi. The market's bustling ambiance and numerous food selections make it an ideal spot for a quick and pleasant family supper.

Frankfurter Botschaft, Westhafenplatz 6-8, 60327 Frankfurt am Main.

Website address: www.frankfurterbotschaft.de.

Café Extrablatt, Kaiserstraße 31, 60329 Frankfurt am Main.

Website: www.cafe-extrablatt.de.

Paulaner am Dom, Domplatz 6, 60311 Frankfurt am Main.

Website address: www.paulaner-am-dom.de

Frankfurter Markthalle, Hasengasse 5-7, 60311 Frankfurt am Main.

Website: www.frankfurtermarkthalle.de.

Children-Friendly Events and Festivals

Frankfurt has a number of child-friendly events and festivals throughout the year, providing fun and entertainment for the entire family. One of the attractions is the Mainfest, a traditional folk festival held in August. The festival includes carnival rides, activities, live music, and food booths. My family liked the joyful atmosphere, riding the attractions, and eating tasty foods like pretzels and cotton candy.

The Frankfurt Christmas Market is another must-see event, especially if you're in town during the holiday season. The market's dazzling decorations, festive booths, and children's activities, like as carousel rides and Santa Claus visits, provide a delightful experience for the entire family.

During the summer, the Opernplatz Festival is a terrific family event. The event takes place in front of the Alte Oper and involves live music, shows, and a variety of food and drink vendors. The colorful and warm atmosphere makes it an enjoyable visit for both youngsters and adults.

The Rheingau Wine Festival, while largely centered on wine, has a variety of activities for families. The event has live music, food vendors, and a children's section with activities and crafts. It's a fantastic opportunity to enjoy the festive atmosphere as the kids are kept busy with numerous activities.

Mainfest website: www.mainfest.de.

Frankfurt Christmas Market website: www.frankfurt-tourismus.de.

Opernplatz Festival (www.opernplatzfest.de)

Rheingau Wine Festival (www.rheingau.com)

Conclusion

Frankfurt is a city full with family-friendly activities, ensuring that tourists of all ages have a memorable and pleasurable time. There are plenty of exciting and interesting activities for families, ranging from touring zoos and animal parks to thrilling rides at amusement parks, interactive museums, and gorgeous parks and playgrounds.

Dining at family-friendly restaurants and attending child-friendly activities and festivals make visiting Frankfurt with children more enjoyable. The city's warm attitude, along with its varied assortment of attractions, makes it an excellent choice for families wishing to build unforgettable experiences.

When planning a family trip to Frankfurt, keep these activities and attractions in mind. Each event brings something unique and adds to the rich tapestry of activities that make Frankfurt such a pleasant destination. Happy exploring!

CHAPTER 10

FOOD AND DINING

Exploring Frankfurt's food scene has been one of the most enjoyable elements of my stay here. The city is a gastronomic melting pot, serving everything from classic German cuisine to cutting-edge culinary inventions. Whether you're eating substantial regional foods, indulging in gourmet experiences, or sampling street food, Frankfurt offers a culinary journey. Here's a comprehensive guide to the foods and dining experiences that make Frankfurt a foodie's dream.

Traditional Frankfurt Cuisine

Frankfurt's traditional food is rich and savory, reflecting the city's cultural legacy and agricultural roots. Grüne Soße (Green Sauce) is one of the most classic foods to taste. This cold herb sauce is produced by combining seven different herbs with sour cream or yogurt and is traditionally served with cooked eggs and potatoes. I first experienced it in Zum Gemalten Haus, a small apple wine bar in Sachsenhausen, and it was a memorable experience. The freshness of the herbs mixed with the creamy smoothness was just delicious.

Another must-try is Frankfurter Würstchen, a sausage comparable to an American hot dog but with a more delicate flavor. These sausages are typically served with mustard and a side of potato salad. I liked them best at Apfelwein Wagner, another old pub that also serves a good range of local apple wine, or Apfelwein.

Apfelwein, a cider-like beverage, is a Frankfurt classic that is best savored in one of the numerous old pubs in Sachsenhausen. The mildly tart beverage is often served in a Bembel (traditional stoneware jug) and poured into ribbed glasses. It's an excellent addition to a hefty dish.

Best Restaurants and Cafes

Frankfurt has a broad selection of restaurants and cafés that appeal to all tastes and budgets. Restaurant Lafleur is a great choice for a sumptuous dining experience. Located in the Palmengarten, this Michelin-starred restaurant serves a menu that combines French and Mediterranean influences with seasonal local foods. The environment is nice, and the food are well prepared. One of my favorite meals here was the Breton lobster, which was well prepared and presented.

Kleinmarkthalle is a must-see for a more relaxed but still enjoyable experience. This thriving indoor market is home to a variety of food vendors and small restaurants. Fresh fruits and cheeses are available, as well as gourmet sandwiches and pastries. I really appreciated the Italian vendor, which had some of the greatest pasta outside of Italy.

If you're searching for a pleasant cafe, Cafe Hauptwache in the center of the city has a delicious combination of classic German cakes and pastries, as well as outstanding coffee. The historic environment adds to the appeal, making it an ideal location for a relaxed getaway.

Street Food & Local Markets

Street food in Frankfurt is a sensory delight, with a wide range of flavors and fragrances drifting through the air. One of the greatest venues to enjoy this is during the Frankfurt Street Food Festival, which takes place many times a year. Gourmet burgers and Asian street cuisine are available here, as are typical German snacks such as bratwurst and pretzels. The festival's bright atmosphere and vast selection of cuisine make it a must-see.

For a more regular street food experience, visit the Berger Strasse Market, which takes place every Wednesday and Saturday. This market has an excellent range of local and foreign street cuisine, fresh vegetables, and handcrafted items. I adored the Turkish stand, which offered delectable gözleme (stuffed flatbread), and the smell of freshly baked items from the bakery shops was intoxicating.

Wine & Beer Tasting

Frankfurt and the adjacent Rhine-Main area are well-known for their wines, especially Riesling. One of the greatest venues to try these wines is at the Rheingau Wine Festival, which takes place every August. This event, held on the Freßgass (Große Bockenheimer Straße), highlights wines from the adjacent Rheingau area. Walking from stall to stall, I drank a diverse range of superb wines, each with its own distinct flavor character. The event also includes live music and food vendors, resulting in a vibrant and happy environment.

For beer aficionados, the Frankfurt Beer Festival, held in June, celebrates artisan beers from Germany and throughout the world. The event offers an extensive assortment of beers, ranging from classic German brews to new craft beers. Tasting events and workshops help participants gain a better grasp of the brewing process and different beer styles.

If you want a more personal atmosphere, head to Frankfurt's classic beer gardens, such as Biergarten am Main. On a nice day, sitting by the river with a refreshing drink is a must-do in Frankfurt.

Vegetarian and Vegan Options

Frankfurt is a vegetarian and vegan friendly city, with numerous eateries serving wonderful plant-based alternatives. Vevay, a vegan restaurant with a diverse menu of inventive and healthful food, is one of my favorites. The Buddha Bowl, which includes fresh veggies, grains, and a savory tahini dressing, is a must-try.

Seven Swans, a Michelin-starred vegetarian restaurant, provides a high-end dining experience with a cuisine that highlights seasonal and local foods. The meals are exquisitely presented, and the tastes are both complex and fulfilling. The setting, in a historic narrow house overlooking the Main River, enhances the eating experience.

For a more casual dinner, Green Karma has a great range of vegan sandwiches, bowls, and smoothies. The freshness and quality of the ingredients make it an excellent choice for a nutritious and flavorful supper.

Food Festivals

Frankfurt organizes many food festivals throughout the year, each highlighting a particular facet of the city's culinary culture. The Green Sauce Festival, held every May, celebrates the city's famed Grüne Soße. The festival includes cooking competitions, tastings, and live music. It's an excellent opportunity to try several sauce versions and vote on your favorite.

The Apple Wine Festival, held in August, honors Frankfurt's distinctive beverage. The event takes place in the Römerberg and features a selection of apple wines from local producers, as well as traditional food, music, and dancing. The cheerful mood and the opportunity to sample several apple wines make it a summer highlight.

The Frankfurt Christmas Market, one of Germany's oldest and largest, is a culinary feast, with stalls selling a wide range of seasonal goodies. The market is a sensory feast, offering everything from roasted chestnuts and gingerbread to substantial sausages and mulled wine.

Cooking Classes

Taking a cooking class is an excellent opportunity to immerse yourself in local food culture while also learning new culinary skills. Cooking Time, located in the center of Frankfurt, provides a variety of programs that include both traditional German cuisine and foreign delicacies. The sessions are hands-on, and the professors are both competent and interesting. One of my favorite sessions was on how to make traditional German sausages, where we studied everything from seasoning the meat to packing the casings.

Kochschule am Westend is another fantastic choice, with lessons ranging from preparing German bread to cooking gourmet cuisine. The sessions are engaging and offer an excellent opportunity to meet other food aficionados. The finest part is sharing the dinner you've made with your peers.

Taste Academy provides innovative wine and food matching lessons. These seminars teach you how to mix local wines with various types of cuisine, increasing your awareness and enthusiasm for both.

Cooking Time (www.cooking-time.de)

Kochschule im Westend (www.kochschule-im-westend.de)

Taste Academy (www.taste-academy.de)

Conclusion

Frankfurt's culinary scene is as varied and lively as the city itself. Whether you're enjoying traditional meals in a quaint pub, discovering the dynamic street food scene, or indulging in a gourmet dinner at a Michelin-starred restaurant, the city has a wide range of eating options to suit all tastes and interests.

The wine and beer festivals, lively markets, and creative vegetarian and vegan alternatives all contribute to Frankfurt's diverse culinary culture. Cooking workshops and food festivals provide more in-depth insights into local culinary traditions, as well as hands-on learning opportunities.

As you explore Frankfurt's food and eating scene, take the time to relish each experience, try new flavors, and learn about the city's diverse culinary legacy. Bon appétit and pleasant dinner!

CHAPTER 11

SHOPPING IN FRANKFURT

Exploring Frankfurt's broad shopping scene was one of the pleasures of my trips to this dynamic city. Frankfurt's shopping options range from vibrant neighborhood markets to high-end designer stores, catering to every taste and budget. Whether you're looking for unusual souvenirs, fashionable clothing, or rare antiques, the city's shopping options provide something for everyone. Here's a detailed guide to the top locations to shop in Frankfurt.

Local Markets and Bazaars

Visiting Frankfurt's lively markets is one of the greatest ways to immerse yourself in the local culture. The Kleinmarkthalle, located near the Zeil commercial district, is a foodie's heaven. This indoor market features over 60 merchants providing fresh fruit, meats, cheeses, and baked delicacies. The fragrances of fresh bread, spices, and flowers permeate the air, providing a sensual experience. I enjoyed walking the aisles, trying local specialties, and speaking with the pleasant merchants. Make sure to taste the area delicacies, such as Handkäse (sour milk cheese) and Frankfurt green sauce.

Another market worth seeing is the Konstablerwache Farmers Market, which takes place every Thursday and Saturday. This outdoor market offers a diverse selection of fresh fruits and vegetables, specialty cheeses, meats, and baked products. The colorful ambiance and high-quality produce make it a neighborhood favorite. I especially appreciated the organic items and handmade jams and preserves.

The Frankfurter Flohmarkt (Frankfurt Flea Market), held every other Saturday along the banks of the Main River, offers a one-of-a-kind shopping experience. This market is a wonderful mine for bargain seekers, selling everything from old clothing and antiques to books and vinyl recordings. The joy of discovering hidden treasures among the varied mix of objects was an adventure in itself.

Kleinmarkthalle, Hasengasse 5-7, 60311 Frankfurt am Main.

Konstablerwache Farmers Market Address: Konstablerwache, 60313 Frankfurt am Main

Frankfurter Flohmarkt: Schaumainkai, 60594 Frankfurt am Main.

Shopping Malls and Centres

Frankfurt's retail malls and complexes provide a contemporary and comfortable shopping experience, with a diverse selection of stores under one roof. MyZeil, located on Zeil Shopping Street, is one of the most popular places. This futuristic mall has a stunning glass façade and an expansive internal design. Inside, you'll discover a mix of worldwide fashion labels, technology businesses, and specialized shops. The food court on the top floor provides a range of eating alternatives with panoramic views of the city. I frequently found myself exploring the most recent fashion trends at Zara and H&M, followed by a soothing coffee at one of the cafés.

Skyline Plaza, located in the Europaviertel area, is another excellent retail destination. This mall has around 170 stores, including prominent brands such as Primark, Mango, and Hollister. The rooftop garden, with its breathtaking views of the Frankfurt skyline, is ideal for taking a breather from shopping. The mall also features a wellness center with spa services and a workout area.

Goethestraße is Frankfurt's most luxurious retail boulevard. This lovely boulevard is lined with luxury boutiques and designer businesses, including Louis Vuitton, Gucci, and Prada. Window shopping here feels like walking through an open-air high fashion exhibition. Even if you don't intend to purchase, it's worth stopping by to see the magnificent stores and soak in the rich ambiance.

MyZeil: Zeil 106, 60313 Frankfurt am Main.

Skyline Plaza: Europa Allee 6, 60327 Frankfurt am Main.

Address: Goethestraße, 60313 Frankfurt am Main.

Souvenir Shops

No vacation to Frankfurt is complete without purchasing some unique souvenirs to commemorate your visit. The Römerberg region, with its historical appeal, is an excellent spot to find traditional gifts. Frankfurt Souvenirs, for example, sells postcards and magnets, as well as handcrafted pottery and regional delicacies. I spotted some wonderfully painted beer steins and traditional wooden toys that would make excellent gifts for friends and family.

The Palais Quartier retail area offers more premium souvenirs. Käthe Wohlfahrt, for example, specializes in traditional German Christmas ornaments and decorations. The detailed craftsmanship and festive ambiance of the store provided for an enjoyable shopping experience. I couldn't resist purchasing a stunningly carved nutcracker and a hand-painted Christmas decoration.

If you enjoy local foods, the Kleinmarkthalle is an excellent spot to purchase tasty keepsakes. Regional items like as apple wine, Frankfurt green sauce, and locally made honey make for memorable and tasty presents.

Frankfurt Souvenirs: Römerberg, 60311 Frankfurt am Main.

Käthe Wohlfahrt: Palais Quartier, Große Eschenheimer Straße 10, 60313, Frankfurt am Main.

Kleinmarkthalle, Hasengasse 5-7, 60311 Frankfurt am Main.

Designer Boutiques

Frankfurt's designer shops provide a carefully chosen collection of high-end apparel and accessories. Lodenfrey, located on Goethestraße, is a premium apparel boutique that sells designer labels like as Dolce & Gabbana, Valentino, and Balenciaga. The store's exquisite design and customized service make shopping here an unforgettable experience.

Another boutique worth seeing is Pfüller Kids & Teens, a high-end children's clothes store that sells fashionable and high-quality children's clothing. The store's tastefully designed displays and rare goods make it a popular choice among trendy parents.

Theresa on Kaiserstraße is a must-see for anyone interested in modern fashion. This store sells stylish and elegant apparel from brands such as Isabel Marant, Chloé, and Saint Laurent. The store's stylish and simple décor enhances the whole shopping experience.

Lodenfrey: Goethestraße 31–33, 60313 Frankfurt am Main.

Pfüller Kids & Teens, Goethestraße 17, 60313 Frankfurt am Main.

Theresa: Kaiserstraße 9, 60311 Frankfurt am Main.

Antiques and Collectibles

Collectors and others hunting for unusual and old goods may find treasures at Frankfurt's antique stores and marketplaces. Antikhaus Insam, located in the Sachsenhausen area, is one of my favorite antique shops. This beautiful boutique sells a well chosen collection of antiques, including furniture, ceramics, and silver. The owner's enthusiasm for antiques is reflected in the quality and range of goods on show. I discovered a lovely vintage clock and a set of exquisite china teacups, which now take pride of place in my house.

The Frankfurt Flea Market is another great spot to look for antiques and treasures. This market, held every other Saturday along the banks of the Main River, sells a variety of products, including vintage clothes, jewelry, antique furniture, and books. The joy of discovering hidden treasures among the varied mix of objects was an adventure in itself.

Kunst- und Auktionshaus Wiesbaden is a must-see destination for art and antique fans. This auction house, located just a short train trip from Frankfurt, has frequent auctions for fine art, antiques, and collectibles. Attending an auction here is a fascinating event, and you may perhaps walk away with a unique and costly object.

Antikhaus Insam, Schweizer Straße 18, 60594 Frankfurt am Main.

Frankfurt Flea Market: Schaumainkai, 60594 Frankfurt am Main.

Kunst- und Auktionshaus Wiesbaden: Sonnenberger Straße 39, 65193 Wiesbaden.

Bookstores and Specialty Shops

For book enthusiasts, Frankfurt has numerous outstanding bookstores with a diverse selection of literature in both German and English. Hugendubel, located on Zeil Shopping Street, is one of Frankfurt's largest bookshops. The store has numerous floors of books, ranging from fiction and nonfiction to travel guides and children's literature. I frequently spent hours exploring the large assortment and sipping coffee in the pleasant in-store café.

Schaulade, a quaint small bookstore in the West End, is another hidden gem. This store focuses on art literature, design, and architecture, making it a sanctuary for art enthusiasts. The well chosen assortment and skilled personnel make it a great location to explore new books and have stimulating talks.

For music fans, No.2 Records is a must-see. This specialist shop in the Bornheim area has a great range of vinyl records, CDs, and music memorabilia. The store's broad assortment includes vintage rock and jazz as well as modern indie and techno music. I loved looking through the record bins and talking with the proprietor, who knows a lot about music.

Feinkost Dallmayr is a gourmet food shop that sells a variety of high-quality delicacies such as chocolate, coffee, and premium wines. The shop's attractive environment and great assortment of items make it an ideal location for picking up delicious presents or treating yourself to something special.

Hugendubel: Zeile 83, 60313 Frankfurt am Main.

Schaulade: Grüneburgweg 92, 60323 Frankfurt am Main.

No. 2 Records: Berger Straße 70, 60316 Frankfurt am Main.

Feinkost Dallmayr, Große Bockenheimer Straße 19, 60313 Frankfurt am Main.

Conclusion

Frankfurt's retail culture is as broad and active as the city itself, with a wide range of experiences to suit everyone's preferences and interests. Whether you're browsing the colorful local markets, indulging in luxury shopping on Goethestraße, or looking for antiques and treasures, Frankfurt offers a rewarding and delightful shopping experience.

The city's mix of sophisticated shopping malls, quaint little boutiques, and lively markets offers countless opportunity to find unique things and immerse yourself in local culture. As you tour Frankfurt's shopping districts, take the time to enjoy each experience, interact with the friendly sellers, and discover the treasures that make this city a shopper's dream.

Happy shopping!

CHAPTER 12

NIGHTLIFE & ENTERTAINMENT

Frankfurt genuinely comes alive after dark, with a dynamic and diversified nightlife that appeals to all preferences. From small pubs and frenetic nightclubs to live music venues and sophisticated theaters, the city has something for everyone who enjoys a good night. During my stay in Frankfurt, I've had the opportunity to explore the city's whole nightlife and entertainment scene, and I'm delighted to share some of my favorites.

Bars & Pubs

Frankfurt's bar culture is as diverse as the city, ranging from classic German taverns to fashionable cocktail bars. One of my favorite places is Apfelwein Wagner in the Sachsenhausen neighborhood. This classic apple wine bar is the ideal spot to begin the evening with a glass of Apfelwein (apple wine), Frankfurt's hallmark drink. The rustic environment, complete with wooden tables and a warm ambiance, exudes genuine local charm. For a truly Frankfurt experience, pair your drink with robust regional delicacies such as Handkäse with Musik (cheese with onions) or Frankfurter Rippchen (pork chops).

For a more modern atmosphere, visit The Parlour, a hidden gem noted for its artisan drinks. This speakeasy-style bar in the Bahnhofsviertel area provides an intimate environment as well as a skillfully created cocktail menu. The mixologists here are truly artists, and seeing them craft custom drinks is a delight in and of itself. I especially liked their trademark drink, which mixed local apple wine with interesting herbal infusions.

Another excellent choice is Old Fritz, a small bar in the Westend neighborhood. This tavern features a pleasant and welcoming ambiance, a diverse assortment of German beers, and a friendly audience. It's a fantastic location to relax and talk with locals or other travelers over a pint.

Apfelwein Wagner, Schweizer Straße 71, 60594 Frankfurt am Main.

The Parlor: Niddastraße 58, 60329 Frankfurt am Main.

Old Fritz: Grüneburgweg 35, 60322 Frankfurt am Main.

Nightclubs and Dance Venues

Frankfurt's party culture is famous, with some of Europe's top nightclubs calling the city home. One of the most well-known is Robert Johnson, which is located in Offenbach, a short drive from Frankfurt. This club is a paradise for electronic music fans, with top-tier DJs and an intimate atmosphere that ensures an amazing experience. The club's position on the banks of the Main River contributes to its distinctive attractiveness.

For a more popular clubbing experience, Gibson Club on the Zeil is an excellent choice. This club has a cutting-edge sound system, attractive design, and a roster of international DJs. On weekends, the dance floor fills up quickly, producing an electrifying environment that keeps you dancing till the early hours.

If you're searching for something unique, Silk Club provides a luxury evening experience. This upmarket club in the middle of Frankfurt has magnificent decor, VIP rooms, and a stylish audience. The music varies from dance and techno to R&B and hip-hop, appealing to a wide audience.

Robert Johnson: Nordring 131, 63067 Offenbach am Main.

Gibson Club, Zeil 85-93, 60313 Frankfurt am Main.

Silk Club, Kaiserstraße 39, 60329 Frankfurt am Main.

Live Music and Concerts

Frankfurt's live music culture is robust and diverse, ranging from classical performances to indie rock gigs. The Alte Oper (Old Opera House) is one of the city's top classical music venues. This magnificent structure accommodates concerts by world-class orchestras, opera singers, and soloists. Attending a performance here is a genuinely amazing experience, with the majesty of the edifice adding to the beauty of the music.

For jazz fans, the Jazzkeller is a must-see. This historic institution has been a cornerstone of Frankfurt's jazz scene since the 1950s, attracting great performers from all over the world. The compact environment and high-quality performances make it popular among both residents and visitors. I spent many hours here, attracted by the wonderful music and vibrant environment.

If you enjoy rock, indie, or alternative music, Batschkapp is the place to be. This iconic club showcases a diverse spectrum of live performers, including up-and-coming bands and veteran musicians. Every performance is a memorable experience because to the crowd's excitement and the sound quality. The club's location in the industrial Nordweststadt district contributes to its edgy appeal.

Alte Oper: Opernplatz 1, 60313 Frankfurt am Main.

Jazzkeller, Kleine Bockenheimer Straße 18a, 60313 Frankfurt am Main.

Batschkapp, Gwinnerstraße 5, 60388 Frankfurt am Main.

Theatres and Cinemas

Frankfurt's cultural landscape is brimming with theaters and cinemas that host a wide variety of shows and films. The Schauspiel Frankfurt is one of the city's premier theaters, recognized for its inventive presentations of both classic and modern plays. The acting quality and ingenuity of the stage design are consistently impressive. I really appreciated their modern interpretation of Shakespeare's "Hamlet," which was both thought-provoking and artistically gorgeous.

For English-speaking guests, the English Theatre Frankfurt is an excellent choice. As Europe's largest English-speaking theater, it presents a diverse selection of English-language plays and musicals. The compact atmosphere and high-quality shows make it a cultural treasure in Frankfurt. I had the pleasure of witnessing "The Importance of Being Earnest" here, and the presentation was both amusing and delightful.

Metropolis Kino is a popular option among moviegoers. This ancient cinema, near the Eschenheimer Tower, shows a mix of mainstream and indie films, frequently in their native language. The iconic art deco decor provides a sense of nostalgia to the moviegoing experience. CineStar Metropolis, in a more modern setting, shows the biggest blockbusters in a pleasant, cutting-edge atmosphere.

Schauspiel Frankfurt: Willy Brandt-Platz 1, 60311 Frankfurt am Main.

English Theatre Frankfurt: Gallusanlage 7, 60329 Frankfurt am Main.

Metropolis Kino, Eschenheimer Anlage 40, 60318 Frankfurt am Main.

CineStar Metropolis, Eschenheimer Anlage 40, 60318 Frankfurt am Main.

Casinos & Gaming

For those who appreciate the thrill of gaming, Frankfurt has numerous fantastic casinos. The Casino Bad Homburg, located in the adjacent spa town of Bad Homburg, is one of Germany's most exquisite and historically significant casinos. With its massive architecture and beautiful atmosphere, it provides a refined gaming experience. The casino offers a variety of games, such as roulette, blackjack, poker, and slot machines. Even if you don't gamble, the ambiance and grandeur of the site make it worthwhile to attend.

Back in Frankfurt, Spielbank Frankfurt provides a more contemporary casino experience. Located in the Westend neighborhood, this casino offers a range of table games and slot machines in a clean and modern atmosphere. The courteous personnel and relaxing environment make it an ideal spot to test your luck.

The Main Tower Casino offers a unique gaming experience. Located on the lower floors of the Main Tower skyscraper, this casino provides breathtaking views of the city as well as a variety of gambling opportunities. The mix of a high-energy environment and beautiful sights results in an amazing evening.

Casino Bad Homburg, Kisseleffstraße 36, 61348 Bad Homburg vor der Höhe

Spielbank Frankfurt, Eschenheimer Tor 2, 60318 Frankfurt am Main.

Main Tower Casino, Neue Mainzer Straße 52-58, 60311 Frankfurt am Main.

Evening Cruises

An nighttime boat down the Main River is a lovely opportunity to observe Frankfurt's skyline while also relaxing. Primus-Linie, a well-known cruise business, provides a number of nighttime excursions that highlight the city's lit monuments. One of my favorite cruises was the dinner cruise, which included a fantastic multi-course meal served on board while we cruised by the shimmering metropolis. The mix of superb meals and breathtaking vistas made for an unforgettable evening.

The After Work Cruise is ideal for those looking for a more relaxed experience. These shorter cruises include live music, beverages, and refreshments, making them ideal for unwinding after a long day. Watching the sun drop over the river and the city lights come to life was a magnificent experience.

Primus Line: Mainkai 36, 60311 Frankfurt am Main.

Website: www.primus-linie.de.

Comedy and Cabaret

Frankfurt's comedy and cabaret scene is vibrant and enjoyable, with a variety of acts to suit diverse tastes. The Künstlerhaus Mousonturm is a cultural facility that presents a wide range of acts, including cabaret, comedy, and experimental theater. The inventive and frequently avant-garde shows here are consistently thought-provoking and entertaining. One of the highlights of my trip was a cabaret performance that was both humorous and caustic about present politics.

For stand-up comedy, the Comedy Hall in the Bornheim area is a popular choice. The intimate environment and excellent comedians make for an enjoyable and laughter-filled evening. The club frequently hosts both local and foreign comedians, resulting in a diverse and entertaining presentation.

The Galli Theater is another excellent venue for comedic and participatory performances. The theater focuses on improvisational humor and participatory presentations that involve the audience. I saw a comedy act here that had the entire crowd laughing, owing to the artists' quick wit and improvisational talents.

Künstlerhaus Mousonturm, Waldschmidtstraße 4, 60316 Frankfurt am Main.

Comedy Hall: Alt-Bornheim 32, 60385 Frankfurt am Main.

Galli Theater, Hamburger Allee 45, 60486 Frankfurt am Main.

Conclusion

Frankfurt's nightlife and entertainment scene is as broad and vibrant as the city itself. From quiet pubs and fashionable nightclubs to live music venues and exquisite theaters, the city has a plethora of possibilities for an unforgettable evening. Frankfurt offers an exceptional experience, whether you're drinking apple wine in a traditional pub, dancing the night away at a renowned nightclub, or watching a live concert or theater play.

Casinos, nighttime cruises, and a thriving comedy and cabaret scene all contribute to the city's diverse nightlife offerings, ensuring that there is something for everyone. As you explore Frankfurt's nightlife and entertainment options, take the time to relish each experience, interact with the people, and immerse yourself in the lively energy that brings this city to life after dark.

Happy exploring!

CHAPTER 13

WELLNESS AND RELAXATION

Frankfurt, with its vibrant city life and fast-paced energy, provides several options for relaxation and renewal. During my visit, I realized that the city has a wide range of wellness and relaxation alternatives to meet any demand, from opulent spas and thermal baths to tranquil yoga retreats and wellness resorts. Let me show you some of the greatest spots to relax and refresh in Frankfurt.

Spa and Wellness Centres

One of the highlights of my Frankfurt health vacation was a visit to the Jumeirah Hotel spa. Located in the center of the city, this magnificent spa provides a variety of treatments to help you rest and revitalize. The mood is tranquil, with soft lighting and pleasant music providing a relaxing atmosphere. I had a full-body massage, which left me feeling fully invigorated. The spa also has a sauna, steam room, and a relaxation area where you may unwind following your treatment.

Another wonderful alternative is the Villa Kennedy Spa, which is part of the Rocco Forte Hotels. This beautiful spa blends modern luxury and traditional therapeutic approaches. I really appreciated the herbal bath and hot stone massage, which both gave profound relaxation. The spa's stunning setting, with its verdant courtyard and quiet ambiance, provided an ideal respite from the city's hustle and bustle.

The Meridian Spa & Fitness at the Skyline Plaza provides a more accessible yet equally soothing experience with a variety of wellness services. This complete wellness center features a spa section with saunas, steam tubs, and a saltwater pool. The treatments vary from traditional massages to more specialized therapies such as Ayurvedic treatments and facials. I had a wonderful time here, traveling from the sauna to the pool and receiving a refreshing facial treatment.

Jumeirah Hotel Spa, Thurn-und-Taxis-Platz 2, 60313 Frankfurt am Main.

Villa Kennedy Spa, Kennedyallee 70, 60596 Frankfurt am Main.

Meridian Spa & Fitness: Europa Allee 4-6, 60327 Frankfurt am Main.

Hot Springs & Thermal Baths

Frankfurt also has some great hot springs and thermal spas, which provide therapeutic advantages and profound relaxation. The Kaiser-Friedrich-Therme in adjacent Wiesbaden is a stunning Art Nouveau bathhouse with a variety of hot pools, saunas, and health services. The ancient building, along with the mineral-rich waters, provide a one-of-a-kind and refreshing experience. I loved bathing in the warm thermal pools and wandering between the several saunas, each of which provided a distinct sensation.

Another excellent choice is the Taunus Therme in Bad Homburg. This huge health facility includes indoor and outdoor hot pools, saunas, and a spa area. The outdoor pool, surrounded by gorgeous flowers, was very calming. The hot waters, which are recognized for their therapeutic capabilities, relieved my stress and left me feeling rejuvenated. The Taunus Therme also provides a variety of health services, including massages and cosmetic therapies.

Kaiser-Friedrich-Therme: Langgasse 38-40, 65183 Wiesbaden.

Taunus Therme Address: Seedammweg 10, 61352 Bad Homburg vor der Höhe

Yoga and Meditation Retreats

For those looking for a more spiritual and holistic approach to wellbeing, Frankfurt has numerous outstanding yoga and meditation retreats. One of my favorite places is the Balance Yoga Institute, which is located in the city center. This facility provides a diverse selection of yoga courses, including energetic Vinyasa flow and soothing Yin yoga. The teachers are highly skilled and provide a pleasant atmosphere for students of all skill levels. Their meditation classes were extremely grounded and relaxing, giving an excellent counterweight to the city's hectic pace.

Yoga Vidya Frankfurt is another excellent option, with a wide range of Hatha yoga, meditation, and Ayurvedic programs and seminars on offer. The peaceful studio and experienced teachers made my lessons here really beneficial. They also provide weekend retreats and seminars, which are ideal for delving further into your practice and obtaining a condition of calm and inner peace.

For a really immersed experience, the Yoga Loft Frankfurt provides retreats and intensive programs that mix yoga, meditation, and wellness treatments. Their retreat facility, located just outside of the city, is placed in a serene natural location, giving it a great spot to unwind and recharge.

Balance Yoga Institute: Oeder Weg 43, 60318 Frankfurt am Main.

Yoga Vidya Frankfurt, Waldschmidtstraße 19, 60316 Frankfurt am Main.

Yoga Loft Frankfurt address: Darmstädter Landstraße 38, 60594 Frankfurt am Main.

Wellness Resorts

For a comprehensive wellness experience, Frankfurt's surrounding wellness resorts provide exquisite retreats where you can rest and revitalize in style. The Vital Hotel Frankfurt, which is located near Hofheim am Taunus, is a premium resort. This resort has a spa and wellness center that offers thermal baths, saunas, and a variety of treatments. The magnificent environment and complete wellness facilities make it ideal for a weekend getaway. I appreciated the detoxifying body wrap and the tranquil outdoor pool area, which provided stunning views of the surrounding countryside.

Another wonderful option is the Kurpark-Hotel Bad Homburg, located in the lovely Kurpark. This hotel provides a variety of wellness packages, including spa treatments, access to thermal baths, and wellness consultations. The calm park environment, along with the superb spa amenities, resulted in a very restful visit. I really enjoyed the hydrotherapy treatments and individualized wellness programs that encourage rest and regeneration.

For a more complete experience, the Hotel Villa Orange in Frankfurt has wellness packages that include spa treatments, yoga sessions, and healthy food alternatives. This eco-friendly hotel prioritizes sustainability and wellbeing, creating a relaxing and caring environment. The organic spa treatments and wonderful nutritional meals made my stay both invigorating and nourishing.

Vital Hotel Frankfurt, Niederhofheimer Straße 67, 65719 Hofheim am Taunus.

Kurpark-Hotel Bad Homburg: Kaiser Friedrich-Promenade 69-75, 61348 Bad Homburg vor der Höhe

Hotel Villa Orange, Hebelstraße 1, 60318 Frankfurt am Main.

Beauty Treatments and Salons

Frankfurt also has various beauty salons and clinics that provide a variety of services to help you look and feel your best. Douglas Beauty Salon, located in the city center, provides a variety of beauty treatments, such as facials, manicures, pedicures, and cosmetics applications. The skilled service and high-quality items utilized made my time here a relaxing and revitalizing experience.

Dr. Derya Bingöl Aesthetics provides sophisticated cosmetic and dermatological treatments for those seeking more specialist care. Whether you need anti-aging treatments, skin rejuvenation, or cosmetic operations, the clinic offers competent care in a luxury atmosphere. The individualized consultations and cutting-edge treatments enabled me to noticeably enhance the texture and look of my skin.

Beautysalon Nicole, located in the Westend neighborhood, is another excellent choice. This boutique salon provides a variety of treatments, including conventional facials and innovative skincare procedures. The peaceful atmosphere and talented aestheticians made my visit a very enjoyable one. I really appreciated their unique facial, which left my skin looking radiant and invigorated.

Douglas Beauty Salon, Zeil 98-102, 60313 Frankfurt am Main.

Dr. Derya Bingöl Aesthetics: Goethestraße 4, 60313 Frankfurt/Main

Beauty Salon Nicole: Grüneburgweg 29, 60322 Frankfurt am Main.

Relaxation Spots

Frankfurt also has plenty of green spaces and quiet areas where you may rest and unwind. One of my favorite destinations is the Palmengarten, a lovely botanical garden that provides a peaceful respite from the city. The garden has several themed parts, including tropical and desert buildings, rose gardens, and a tranquil lake. Strolling around the lush surroundings and admiring the brilliant blossoms gave an ideal opportunity to unwind and connect with nature.

The Grüneburgpark is another great place to unwind. This vast park features large lawns, shady walks, and a charming Japanese garden. It's ideal for a picnic, a leisurely walk, or just resting on the grass and reading a book. The park's quiet environment and stunning surroundings make it one of my favorite locations to decompress.

Nidda Park, with its enormous playground constructed like a tiny city and wide walking and bike routes, offers a one-of-a-kind experience. The park's natural splendor, along with the tranquil flow of the Nidda River, creates a serene area ideal for leisure and pleasure.

Palmengarten, Siesmayerstraße 61, 60323 Frankfurt am Main.

Grüneburg Park: August-Siebert-Straße, 60323 Frankfurt am Main.

Nidda Park, Am Ginnheimer Wäldchen, 60431 Frankfurt am Main.

Fitness Centres and Gymnasiums

Frankfurt has a number of excellent fitness centers and gyms for folks who appreciate being active. Prime Time Fitness, with many sites around the city, provides cutting-edge facilities, personal training, and a wide range of fitness courses. The latest equipment and experienced coaches helped me stick to my exercise program while abroad. I really appreciated their high-intensity interval training (HIIT) programs, which were both tough and effective.

Another great choice is Fitness First, which has many sites throughout Frankfurt. This gym chain provides extensive workout facilities, such as cardio and strength training equipment, group fitness programs, and wellness spaces with saunas and steam rooms. The welcoming atmosphere and many class offerings, ranging from yoga to spinning, make it simple to keep motivated and active.

Fitseveneleven provides a one-of-a-kind and fashionable training setting for a more upscale fitness experience. This gym blends cutting-edge exercise equipment with a lively and upbeat ambiance. Their class offerings, which included functional training, boxing, and dance, made for a pleasant and diverse exercise experience.

Prime Time Fitness, Börsenstraße 7-11, 60313 Frankfurt am Main.

Fitness First: Zeil 65–69, 60313 Frankfurt am Main

Fitseveneleven, Hanauer Landstraße 147-149, 60314 Frankfurt am Main.

Conclusion

Frankfurt's health and relaxation scene has a wide range of solutions to help you rest, revitalize, and find balance among the city's hectic bustle. The city offers several options for relaxation and self-care, including magnificent spas and thermal baths, as well as tranquil yoga retreats and wellness resorts. The beauty treatments and relaxation locations add to the experience, ensuring that you leave Frankfurt feeling refreshed and invigorated.

Frankfurt's wellness options appeal to all needs and preferences, whether you're indulging in a spa treatment, swimming in thermal waters, doing yoga, or simply relaxing in a botanical garden. Take the time to visit these great destinations and enjoy the relaxing and refreshing pleasures they provide. Your mind, body, and soul will be grateful to you.

Happy relaxation!

CHAPTER 14

SPORT AND OUTDOOR ACTIVITIES

Frankfurt, with its dynamic city life and rich natural environs, provides a plethora of outdoor activities and sports options to suit all interests and fitness levels. During my time in Frankfurt, I made an effort to experience the city's varied choice of outdoor activities, from golfing on immaculate courses to sailing on tranquil waterways. Here's a full introduction to some of the top sports and outdoor activities available in and around Frankfurt.

Golf Courses

One of the best ways to spend a beautiful day in Frankfurt is on the golf course. The city and its surrounds are home to numerous world-class golf courses that provide both demanding play and breathtaking views. The Frankfurter

Golf Club, located in the Niederrad area, is one of Germany's oldest and most distinguished clubs. Established in 1913, this club has a nicely kept 18-hole course that weaves through lush fairways and thick trees. The course is both difficult and pleasant, with strategically placed bunkers and water hazards to challenge your abilities. After a game of golf, the clubhouse provides a comfortable setting to unwind and enjoy a meal or a drink.

Another fantastic alternative is Golfpark Bachgrund, which is located just south of Frankfurt. This club has a 27-hole championship course that accommodates players of all ability levels. The course is nestled among rolling hills and stunning scenery, making it an idyllic backdrop for a round of golf. The club also has a driving range, practice areas, and a pro shop. I really appreciated the friendly and casual attitude, which contributed to a wonderful and memorable golfing experience.

Golfclub Hanau-Wilhelmsbad provides a more informal and accessible option, with a magnificent 18-hole course that is appropriate for both beginners and expert golfers. The course is nestled in a historic parkland and features tree-lined fairways and well-kept greens. The club also provides golf instruction and seminars, so it's an excellent location to hone your talents.

Frankfurter Golf Club address: Golfstraße 41, 60528 Frankfurt am Main.

Golf Park Bachgrund: Gernsheimer Landstraße 60, 64560 Riedstadt.

Golf Club Hanau-Wilhelmsbad: Lamboystraße 52, 63452 Hanau.

Horseback Riding

For individuals who enjoy horses and the beautiful outdoors, Frankfurt has numerous good horseback riding options. Reitstall Hofgut Liederbach, located just outside of the city, is an excellent area to go horseback riding in a gorgeous rural environment. The stables provide riding lessons for all skill levels, from beginners to expert riders, as well as guided trail rides through the picturesque countryside. The well-trained horses and competent teachers provide a safe and fun riding experience. I really appreciated the trail rides, which brought us through beautiful meadows and woodlands, giving a peaceful getaway from the city.

Another excellent alternative is Reitstall am Domhof, which is located near Kronberg. This equestrian center provides a variety of riding activities, such as dressage, show jumping, and leisure riding. The building is well-maintained, and the employees are polite and informed. Whether you want to enhance your riding abilities or simply enjoy a relaxing ride, this facility provides something for you.

For a more thorough experience, Reit- und Fahrverein Frankfurt provides extensive riding programs such as lessons, trail rides, and equestrian contests. The club's facilities are first-rate, and the emphasis on safety and instruction makes it an ideal destination for riders of all ages.

Reitstall Hofgut Liederbach: Hofgut 1, 65835 Liederbach am Taunus.

Reitstall am Domhof, Hainstraße 25, 61476 Kronberg am Taunus.

Reit- und Fahrverein Frankfurt, Wilhelm-Epstein-Straße 2, 60431 Frankfurt am Main.

Sailing and Boating

Frankfurt's closeness to the Main River and other neighboring lakes affords several options for sailors and boaters. The Frankfurt Sailing Club, located on the banks of the Main River, provides a variety of sailing activities and courses for all skill levels. The club's welcoming atmosphere and picturesque river setting make it an ideal venue to learn and enjoy sailing. I attended a beginner's sailing lesson here, and the experience was both informative and exciting. The experience of sailing the river with the wind in my sails was simply amazing.

Nidda Park rents out pedal boats and rowboats on the peaceful Nidda River for a more leisurely boating experience. This is an excellent pastime for families and people wishing to spend a relaxing day on the lake. The park's natural splendor and the steady flow of the river create a peaceful setting for a leisurely boat trip.

If you prefer more daring water activities, Lake Langener Waldsee, just outside Frankfurt, is a popular destination for sailing, windsurfing, and paddleboarding. The lake's clean waters and well-maintained amenities make it a popular choice for water sports aficionados. I had an amazing day windsurfing here, and the friendly atmosphere and outstanding instructors made it both enjoyable and rewarding.

Frankfurt Sailing Club, Gerbermühlstraße 1, 60594 Frankfurt am Main.

Nidda Park, Am Ginnheimer Wäldchen, 60431 Frankfurt am Main.

Lake Langener Waldsee: Am Seehafen 1, 63225 Langen.

Fishing Spots

For those who appreciate fishing, Frankfurt has numerous great places to cast a line and relax by the lake. The Main River is a famous fishing spot for a variety of fish species, including pike, perch, and carp. The river's banks provide countless opportunities for both recreational and serious fisherman. One of my favorite fishing sites is near the Eiserner Steg, where the calm waters and picturesque vistas of the city provide for an ideal environment for a leisurely day of fishing.

Another excellent fishing spot is Lake Nidda, which is located in Nidda Park. The lake is well-stocked with fish and provides a tranquil setting for fishing. The park's attractions, such as picnic sites and walking pathways, make it an ideal place to spend a day outside with family and friends. I appreciated the lake's peaceful and quiet setting, which made fishing a genuinely enjoyable experience.

For a more rustic fishing experience, the Schwarzbach River near Bad Vilbel is a hidden treasure. This little river is well-known for its beautiful waters and abundance of fish, particularly trout and grayling. The surrounding countryside offers a magnificent and tranquil setting for fishing. The local fishing community is friendly and may provide important suggestions and advice for getting the most out of your fishing excursion.

Main River: Various spots along the riverbanks of Frankfurt.

Lake Nidda, Am Ginnheimer Wäldchen, 60431 Frankfurt am Main.

Schwarzbach River is near Bad Vilbel, Hesse.

Tennis and Sport Clubs

Frankfurt has a variety of sports clubs and facilities where you may practice tennis and other physical activities. The Tennis Club Palmengarten, located in the city center, is one of Frankfurt's oldest and most prominent tennis clubs. The club has well-maintained clay courts, a clubhouse, and a welcoming community of tennis lovers. Whether you want to play a casual match or compete in a league, this club has great facilities and a friendly atmosphere.

Another excellent alternative is the Tennis- und Hockey-Club (THC) Hanau, which is located just outside Frankfurt. This club provides a variety of sporting activities, including tennis, field hockey, and fitness courses. The contemporary facilities and professional teaching team make it an excellent location to hone your talents while being active. I especially appreciated the group tennis sessions, which were a pleasant and sociable method to improve my game.For those seeking a more full sports club experience, the Frankfurter Turnverein 1860 (FTV 1860) provides a variety of activities such as tennis, basketball, gymnastics, and swimming. The club's enormous facilities and numerous programming welcome members of all ages and fitness levels. The warm community and many sports offerings make it an ideal place to keep active and meet new people.

Tennis Club Palmengarten, Palmengartenstraße 11, 60325 Frankfurt am Main.

Tennis and Hockey Club Hanau: Am Tennisplatz 1, 63452 Hanau.

Frankfurter Turnverein 1860, Eschersheimer Landstraße 248, 60320 Frankfurt am Main.

Hiking and Bike Trails

Frankfurt's natural surroundings provide a multitude of hiking and bicycling routes suitable for all levels of outdoor lovers. The Taunus Mountains, immediately north of the city, offer some of the greatest hiking options in the area. The Großer Feldberg, the highest summit in the Taunus, has many well-marked routes that wind through lush forests and provide breathtaking panoramic views. I appreciated the challenge of ascending to the peak, where the spectacular views of the surrounding landscape made the effort worthwhile.

For a more leisurely climb, the Lohrberg near Frankfurt has stunning routes that weave past vineyards and orchards. The stunning views of the city and the Main River make for a nice walk. The top has a park with picnic spaces and a vineyard, making it an ideal site for a picnic and a bottle of local wine.

For bikers, the Main Radweg (Main River Cycle Path) provides an excellent route that follows the Main River from its source to its confluence with the Rhine. The well-maintained trail is excellent for cyclists of all skill levels and provides stunning views of the river and its surroundings. I spent several delightful afternoons riding along this road, stopping at quaint riverfront villages and admiring the scenery along the way.

Taunus Mountains: Several paths, notably Großer Feldberg.

Lohrberg: Lohrbergstraße, 60389 Frankfurt/Main

Main Radweg follows the Main River from its source to its junction with the Rhine.

Water Sports and Activities

Frankfurt's closeness to the Main River and neighboring lakes makes it an excellent choice for water sports aficionados. Stand-up paddleboarding (SUP) on the Main River is a popular pastime that provides an enjoyable and unique way to experience the city from the water. SUP Frankfurt provides rentals and guided trips for all levels of skill. I found paddleboarding to be a pleasant and fun way to observe the city's monuments while also enjoying the quiet of the river.

Lake Langener Waldsee is an excellent location for people who enjoy more extreme water activities. The lake provides options for windsurfing, canoeing, and sailing. The clean waters and well-maintained amenities make it a popular destination for water sports aficionados. I really liked windsurfing on the lake, where the friendly community and outstanding instructors made the experience thrilling and fulfilling.

If you prefer a more relaxing water activity, Nidda Park's rowboat and pedal boat rentals provide a calm way to enjoy the water. The Nidda River's steady flow, along with the magnificent park surrounds, creates a tranquil setting for a relaxing boat trip. This activity is ideal for families and people seeking to relax and reconnect with nature.

SUP Frankfurt: Several places along the Main River.

Lake Langener Waldsee: Am Seehafen 1, 63225 Langen.

Nidda Park, Am Ginnheimer Wäldchen, 60431 Frankfurt am Main.

Conclusion

Frankfurt's varied choice of sports and outdoor activities has something for everyone, from ardent golfers and horseback riders to sailors and hikers. The city's well-kept amenities, stunning natural surroundings, and warm residents make it an ideal location for outdoor enjoyment and exercise.

Whether you're exploring the gorgeous hiking trails of the Taunus Mountains, playing a game of golf on a pristine course, or paddleboarding on the Main River, Frankfurt offers an abundance of chances to keep active and enjoy the great outdoors. Take the time to explore these activities and experience the beauty and adventure that Frankfurt has to offer.

Have fun exploring!

CHAPTER 15

EVENTS & FESTIVALS

Frankfurt is a city that knows how to celebrate, with a calendar jam-packed with festivals and events that represent its diverse cultural heritage and lively community spirit. During my stay in Frankfurt, I had the opportunity to attend some of the city's most memorable and celebratory festivals. Here's a comprehensive guide to the events and festivals that make Frankfurt a city of boundless energy and charm.

Annual Festivals

Frankfurt holds numerous yearly festivals that are major events in the city's cultural calendar. One of the most popular is the Frankfurt Book Fair (Frankfurter Buchmesse), which is held in October. As the world's largest book fair, it attracts publishers, writers, and book fans from all over the world. Wandering around the immense halls of the Messe Frankfurt, I was astounded by the sheer variety of books available and the chance to meet some of my favorite authors. Readings, signings, and conversations make the fair a literary enthusiast's dream come true.

Another notable event is the Frankfurt Christmas Market, which transforms the city into a winter wonderland from late November until December. The market, which is located around the Römerberg and Paulsplatz, has beautifully adorned wooden stalls offering everything from handcrafted presents to delectable snacks like gingerbread and mulled wine. The holiday ambiance, complete with dazzling lights and the sound of carolers, creates a beautiful experience. I liked sipping hot Glühwein while visiting the vendors, experiencing the festive mood all around.

In the summer, the Mainfest is a must-see. This traditional folk festival, held in August, takes place along the Main River's banks. The event has carnival rides, games, live music, and food booths. The fireworks display across the river was a highlight for me, as it lighted up the night sky in a stunning array of colors.

Frankfurt Book Fair website: www.buchmesse.de.

Frankfurt Christmas Market website: www.frankfurt-tourismus.de.

Mainfest website: www.mainfest.de.

Music and Arts Festivals

Frankfurt's music and arts festivals highlight the city's thriving cultural landscape. The Jazz Festival Frankfurt, which takes place in October, is one of the most famous jazz events in Europe. The festival includes concerts by world-renowned jazz musicians in a variety of locations across the city. I went to numerous performances in the Alte Oper and the Jazzkeller, which both provided a great experience of live jazz in intimate and magnificent venues.

The Museumsuferfest, which takes place every August along the Museum Embankment, is another cultural attraction. This event showcases Frankfurt's vibrant museum culture with open-air music, art displays, and performances. The festival environment, which includes food booths and artisan merchants along the riverbank, is colorful and interesting. I enjoyed seeing the museums during the day and listening to music and attending the celebrations at night.

The Frankfurt Art Experience, held in September, is an excellent event for those who enjoy contemporary art. The event will feature exhibitions, gallery visits, and workshops, as well as a forum for known and upcoming artists. This event exudes vitality and originality, and it's an excellent opportunity to immerse oneself in the city's thriving art scene.

Jazz Festival Frankfurt (www.jazzfestivalfrankfurt.de)

Museumsuferfest (www.museumsuferfest.de)

Frankfurt Art Experience (www.frankfurt-artexperience.de)

Cultural and historical Celebrations

Frankfurt's cultural and historical events provide insight into the city's rich background and customs. The Frankfurt Apple Wine Festival, celebrated in August, honors the city's favorite beverage, Apfelwein (apple wine). The event takes place at the Roßmarkt and includes a selection of apple wines from local producers, as well as traditional food, music, and dancing. I liked trying several apple wines and learning about the history and manufacture of this renowned beverage.

The Wäldchestag (Forest Day) is another distinct event that takes place on the Tuesday after Pentecost. This local festival is a centuries-old custom in which Frankfurt residents travel to the city forest for a day of celebration. The woodland is brimming with food booths, beer gardens, and entertainment. It's an excellent opportunity to learn about local traditions and spend the day outside with the community.

Frankfurt Apple Wine Festival (www.frankfurt-tourismus.de)

Wäldchestag: Various places inside the Frankfurt City Forest.

Food and Beverage Festivals

Frankfurt's food and drink festivals are a culinary feast, allowing visitors to enjoy the finest of both local and foreign cuisine. The Rheingau Wine Festival, held in August on the Freßgass (Große Bockenheimer Straße), features wines from the surrounding Rheingau area. The celebration includes wine tastings, food vendors, and live music. While strolling around the Freßgass with a drink of Riesling in hand, I loved finding new wines and sampling excellent culinary combinations.

The Frankfurt Green Sauce Festival, celebrated in May, honors the city's signature cuisine, Grüne Soße (green sauce). The festival features cooking competitions, tastings, and live music. I enjoyed testing several sauce combinations and voting for my favorite. The festival ambiance, with its emphasis on local food and community spirit, made for an enjoyable and engaging event.

For a sample of diverse tastes, the Frankfurt Street Food Festival is a must-see. This event, which takes place many times a year in various places, has a diverse range of street food vendors serving anything from gourmet burgers to exotic Asian cuisine. The colorful environment and diverse cuisine make it a foodie's heaven.

Rheingau Wine Festival (www.rheingau.com)

Frankfurt Green Sauce Festival (www.gruene-sosse-festival.de)

Frankfurt Street Food Festival: Various sites; www.frankfurt-tourismus.de

Sporting Events

Frankfurt's athletic activities are vibrant and diverse, drawing followers from all over the world. The Frankfurt Marathon, which takes place in October, is one of the major events. This marathon is one of the oldest in Germany, attracting thousands of participants. The track leads you through the city's streets, past attractions such as the Römer and the Main River. The atmosphere is exciting, with cheering spectators and live music along the way. Whether you're a participant or a spectator, the Frankfurt Marathon is an exciting event.

The Ironman European Championship, held in July, is another significant athletic event. This strenuous triathlon consists of a swim in the Langener Waldsee, a bike ride over the Taunus Mountains, and a marathon run through Frankfurt's city center. Watching the athletes push their boundaries is motivating, and the city comes alive with enthusiasm and support for the contestants.

For football lovers, attending an Eintracht Frankfurt game at Deutsche Bank Park is a must. The stadium is packed with enthusiastic people roaring on their side. The Bundesliga matches are usually exciting, and seeing them live is an excellent opportunity to immerse oneself in the local sports culture.

Frankfurt Marathon website: www.frankfurt-marathon.com.

Ironman European Championship (www.ironman.com)

Eintracht Frankfurt: Deutsche Bank Park, Mörfelder Landstraße 362, 60528, Frankfurt am Main.

Seasonal Events

Frankfurt's seasonal events capture the essence of each season and provide unique experiences all year. The Spring Dippemess, held in April on the Festplatz am Ratsweg, is one of the city's major folk events. The festival includes carnival rides, games, food booths, and live entertainment. It's a terrific way to kick out the spring season with fun and excitement. I loved the colorful environment, eating traditional festival delicacies like bratwurst and cotton candy, and trying my luck at the games.

In the summer, the Opernplatz Festival, held in June, transforms the area in front of the Alte Oper into a lively open-air arena. The event includes live music, shows, and a variety of food and beverage kiosks. The balmy summer evenings and picturesque backdrop make for a memorable experience. I enjoyed listening to live jazz while sipping a glass of wine and taking in the festive atmosphere.

The Autumn Dippemess, held in September, is a counterpart to the spring festival and has comparable attractions with an emphasis on fall themes. The festival's main attraction is the traditional market, which sells handcrafted goods, local products, and tasty seasonal meals.

Spring Dippemess (www.frankfurt-tourismus.de)

Opernplatz Festival (www.opernplatzfest.de)

Autumn Dippemess: http://www.frankfurt-tourismus.de

Special Interest Events

Frankfurt also conducts a number of special specialty events that appeal to certain audiences and offer unique experiences. Frankfurt Tattoo Convention, held in March, is one of Europe's major tattoo events. The festival brings together tattoo artists and aficionados from all around the world. Attending the conference was a fascinating event, complete with live tattooing, art displays, and the opportunity to meet famous artists.

For auto lovers, the Frankfurt Motor Show (IAA), held every two years in September, is a must-see. This international auto show shows the most recent advances in the automobile industry, including exhibits from major vehicle manufacturers and cutting-edge technology. Walking around the huge exhibition halls, I was astounded by the future concept automobiles and technological advances in electric vehicles.

The Christmas Garden Frankfurt, presented at the Palmengarten, is a wonderful winter event that turns the botanical garden into a sparkling paradise. The lit paths, spectacular light works, and festive atmosphere make for an ideal nighttime adventure. Walking around the garden, surrounded by dazzling lights and seasonal decorations, was a magical experience.

Frankfurt Tattoo Convention (www.frankfurt-tattoo-convention.de)

Frankfurt Motor Show (IAA) website: www.iaa.de

Christmas Garden Frankfurt (www.christmas-garden.de)

Conclusion

Frankfurt's events and festivals reflect the city's rich cultural legacy and robust community spirit. Frankfurt is always buzzing with excitement, from literary celebrations and music festivals to traditional folk gatherings and seasonal festivities. These events give not just entertainment but also a greater understanding of the city's customs, culture, and people.

Whether you're visiting the world's largest book fair, drinking apple wine at a local festival, or rooting for athletes at a major sporting event, Frankfurt's festivals and events offer exceptional experiences. Take the opportunity to participate in these festivals and discover the enthusiasm and energy that make Frankfurt such a vibrant and intriguing city.

Happy celebration!

CHAPTER 16

HISTORIC SITES

Frankfurt is a city in which history and modernity live together. The architecture, museums, and landmarks reflect the city's rich history. During my stay in Frankfurt, I made it a point to see the city's historical sites, which each tell a tale of the city's transformation from a medieval commerce center to a worldwide financial metropolis. Here's a detailed tour to some of Frankfurt's most notable historical landmarks.

Römer & Römerberg

The Römer and Römerberg are at the center of Frankfurt's historic area. The Römer, a medieval edifice that has functioned as the city hall for almost 600 years, is one of Frankfurt's most recognizable buildings. The Römer's façade is readily identifiable, with its gabled roof and medieval design. Walking around the Römerberg, the square in front of the Römer, I was transported back in time. The plaza is surrounded by wonderfully restored half-timbered homes, each with their own distinct character.

One of the pleasures of my Römer tour was seeing the Kaisersaal (Emperor's Hall), where Holy Roman Emperors were formerly crowned. The hall is filled with pictures of all the emperors, creating a strong sense of antiquity. The Römerberg also has the Old St. Nicholas Church, a lovely Gothic chapel dating back to the 13th century. The church's basic yet attractive interior offers a calm respite from the busy square outside.

During my stay, I also heard about the importance of the Frankfurt Christmas Market, which is held in the Römerberg every year. The market is one of Germany's oldest and largest, and the square is alive with Christmas vendors, dazzling lights, and the scent of mulled wine and gingerbread. Even outside of the holiday season, the Römerberg organizes a variety of events and festivals, making it an exciting destination to visit.

Address: Römerberg 27, 60311 Frankfurt am Main.

Frankfurt Cathedral

Another historical building worth visiting is the Frankfurt Cathedral, also known as Kaiserdom St. Bartholomäus. This Gothic cathedral, with its towering spire and commanding presence, has had a profound impact on Frankfurt's history. For over 300 years, the cathedral served as the coronation location for Holy Roman Emperors, and its great architecture and religious ambiance reflect its historical significance.

One of the cathedral's most prominent characteristics is its high altar, which dates from the 15th century and is embellished with elaborate carvings and gold accents. The cathedral's interior is similarly magnificent, with exquisite stained glass windows, elegant chapels, and a sense of devotion throughout.

Climbing the cathedral tower was a highlight of my trip. The climb is difficult, but the panoramic views of Frankfurt from the summit are well worth the effort. From the tower, I could observe the contrast between the medieval old town and the modern skyline, demonstrating Frankfurt's distinct combination of history and development.

The Dommuseum, housed within the cathedral, displays a collection of religious objects, manuscripts, and artworks. The museum gives excellent information about the cathedral's history and position in Frankfurt's religious and cultural life.

Address: Domplatz 1, 60311 Frankfurt am Main.

Website address: www.dom-frankfurt.de.

Goethe House

Johann Wolfgang von Goethe, one of Germany's finest poets, was born at the Goethe House, which is located in the center of Frankfurt. Visiting the Goethe House was like entering the world of the 18th century, when Goethe spent his formative years. The home has been expertly reconstructed to resemble the period's design, with each room providing insight into Goethe's life and the surroundings that inspired his writing talent.

One of the most remarkable elements of the Goethe House is the writer's study, where Goethe wrote some of his first works. The chamber is furnished with period furniture, documents, and personal objects, allowing an intimate glimpse into the life of the young Goethe. The library, which was filled with 18th-century literature, was very striking and provided me with a feeling of Goethe's intellectual surroundings.

The Goethe Museum, located adjacent to the Goethe House, has a collection of artworks, manuscripts, and artifacts relating to Goethe's life and work. The museum's exhibitions promote a fuller understanding of Goethe's contributions to literature, science, and the arts. I particularly like the collection of photographs and personal letters, which brought this literary giant's varied nature to life.

Address: Großer Hirschgraben 23-25, 60311 Frankfurt am Main.

Website: www.goethehaus-frankfurt.de.

Archaeological sites

Frankfurt's rich history is also represented in its archeological sites, which provide an insight into the city's distant past. The Archäologisches Museum Frankfurt houses relics dating back thousands of years, from the Stone Age to the Middle Ages. The museum is located in a former Carmelite convent, which adds to its historical value.

One of the museum's attractions is the Roman Frankfurt display, which features items from the Roman colony of Nida, which is now located in the Heddernheim area. The collection includes ceramics, utensils, jewelry, and a comprehensive model of the Roman town, offering an intriguing glimpse into life in ancient Frankfurt. The Roman bath complex piqued my interest, as did the common artifacts that gave light on the people' daily life.

Another important archaeological site is the Kaiserpfalz Franconofurd, which is located in the old town near the cathedral. This site has the remnants of a Carolingian royal residence from the ninth century. The excavations have discovered foundations, walls, and relics that give important information about the early medieval era. Walking across the grounds, I could visualize the palace's grandeur and significance in Holy Roman Empire history.

Address: Archäologisches Museum Frankfurt, Karmelitergasse 1, 60311, Frankfurt am Main.

Website: www.archaeologisches-museum.frankfurt.de.

Kaiserpfalz Franconofurd, Markt 10, 60311 Frankfurt am Main.

Historic Churches and Cathedrals

Frankfurt is home to numerous old churches and cathedrals that are both architectural wonders and cultural monuments. St. Paul's Church (Paulskirche) is one of the most significant places in German history, as it hosted the first democratically elected German parliament in 1848. The church's neoclassical style and involvement in the democratic revolution make it a symbol of German unity and freedom. The church's interior is basic yet lovely, and the exhibition about the history of the German parliament is both educational and inspiring.

St. Catherine's Church (Katharinenkirche), situated on the Zeil, is another prominent church in Frankfurt. This Baroque church has a magnificent red sandstone façade and is one of the city's largest Protestant churches. The church's interior is similarly spectacular, with stunning stained glass windows, a large organ, and a peaceful ambiance. Attending a service or performance here is an excellent chance to learn about the church's rich cultural and spiritual history.

Alte Nikolaikirche, located in Römerberg, is a lovely Gothic church dating back to the 12th century. The interior of the church is decorated with exquisite murals, a spectacular altar, and an elegantly carved pulpit. The church's carillon, which plays a tune every hour, contributes to the Römerberg's enchanting ambiance.

St. Leonhard's Church (Leonhardskirche) is one of Frankfurt's oldest churches, dating from the 13th century. The church's Romanesque and Gothic architecture, as well as its stunning stained glass windows and historical objects, making it an intriguing place to visit. The church's crypt, which houses the bones of Frankfurt's early Christian martyrs, contributes to its historical value.

St. Paul's Church, Paulsplatz 11, 60311 Frankfurt am Main.

St. Catherine's Church: An der Hauptwache 1, 60313, Frankfurt am Main.

Alte Nikolaikirche, Römerberg 11, 60311 Frankfurt am Main.

St. Leonhard's Church, Leonhardstraße 6, 60313 Frankfurt am Main.

Museums & Exhibitions

Frankfurt's museums and exhibitions offer a comprehensive view of the city's history, art, and culture. The Historisches Museum Frankfurt, located in the Old Town, is a must-see for anybody interested in the city's history. The museum's displays extend from medieval Frankfurt to the current period. One of the attractions is the model of Frankfurt in 1926, which gives a realistic and intriguing look at the city's layout and architecture before to World War II. The museum also has an extraordinary collection of antiques, artworks, and multimedia exhibits that bring Frankfurt's history to life.

The Städel Museum, one of Germany's most renowned art museums, is another must-see site. The museum's collection includes almost 700 years of European art, ranging from the Middle Ages to modern pieces. The gallery's classics include works by Rembrandt, Vermeer, Monet, and Picasso. I spent hours perusing the museum's extensive collection, admiring the artworks' beauty and diversity. The museum's current expansion, which includes contemporary art, provides a vibrant contrast to the historical exhibits.

For a more focused look at Frankfurt's Jewish history, the Jewish Museum Frankfurt is a moving and educational site. The museum, located in the Rothschild Palais, displays exhibits about Jewish life, culture, and history in Frankfurt. The museum's collection contains artifacts, papers, and pictures that give a profound and compelling understanding of the Jewish community's contributions and experiences. The museum's position near the old Jewish ghetto enhances its historical relevance.

The Museum of Modern Art (MMK) is a must-see for contemporary art fans. The museum's collection contains works by prominent contemporary artists and provides a stimulating examination of modern art. The museum's creative design is impressive, and changing exhibitions guarantee that there is always something fresh and intriguing to view.

Historisches Museum Frankfurt, Saalhof 1, 60311 Frankfurt am Main.

Städel Museum: Schaumainkai 63, 60596 Frankfurt am Main.

Jewish Museum Frankfurt, Untermainkai 14/15, 60311 Frankfurt am Main.

Museum of Modern Art (MMK): Domstraße 10, 60311 Frankfurt am Main.

Conclusion

Frankfurt's historical landmarks provide an intriguing trip through time, representing the city's rich and diverse history. From the ancient architecture of the Römer and the stately Frankfurt Cathedral to the literary heritage of the Goethe House and the informative exhibitions at the city's museums, there is a plethora of history to discover.

Each location offers a unique glimpse into Frankfurt's past, whether it's the ancient items at the archeological museum, the inspirational history of St. Paul's Church, or the artistic treasures at the Städel Museum. These historical sites not only convey the tale of Frankfurt, but also provide a better knowledge of the cultural and historical factors that molded the city.

As you visit Frankfurt's historical monuments, take the time to enjoy the intricacies and become immersed in the story they tell. Frankfurt's combination of history, culture, and art is incredibly intriguing, bringing the past and present together in a beautiful and meaningful way.

Happy exploring!

CHAPTER 17

ITINERARY AND SAMPLE PLANS

Frankfurt is a city that has something for everyone, whether you're going for a weekend vacation, looking for cultural immersion, outdoor experiences, traveling with family, on a budget, or seeking a luxury experience. After spending a lot of time seeing Frankfurt, I've put together a series of thorough itineraries to help you get the most out of your stay. Each itinerary is tailored to your interests and travel style, highlighting the best of Frankfurt's offerings.

Weekend Getaway

Day 1: Arrival and Exploration

- Morning, arrive in Frankfurt and check into your hotel. Begin your day with a visit to Römer and Römerberg. Wander around the lovely plaza, admiring the historic buildings and visiting the Old St. Nicholas Church.

- Lunch: Zum Storch Am Dom serves traditional German cuisine and is recognized for its substantial meals and pleasant environment.

- Afternoon: Visit Frankfurt Cathedral. Climb the tower to get panoramic views of the city. Next, visit the adjacent Goethe House to learn about Germany's finest writer.

- Evening: Take a stroll along the Main River and see the skyline. Have supper at MainNizza, which serves wonderful food and has stunning river views.

Day 2: Museums & Shopping

- Morning: Begin with a visit to the Städel museum. Spend a few hours examining the extensive art collection.

- Lunch: Visit the Kleinmarkthalle for a wide variety of cuisine alternatives. Try some local delights.

- Afternoon: Explore Zeil, Frankfurt's largest retail district. Do not miss MyZeil retail mall's modern architecture.

- Evening: Wrap out your weekend with a wonderful lunch at Restaurant Francais, a Michelin-starred restaurant in the center of Frankfurt.

Cultural Immersion

Day 1: Historic Sites

- Morning: Start with a guided tour of the Römer and Römerberg. Learn about the historic importance of these landmarks.

- meal: Enjoy a traditional meal at Apfelwein Wagner while enjoying Frankfurt's famed apple wine.

- Afternoon: Learn more about Frankfurt's history at the Historisches Museum. Spend the remainder of the afternoon touring the exhibitions.

- Evening: Attend a concert at the Alte Oper. The magnificent setting and excellent performers combine for an amazing evening.

Day two: Art and Literature

- Morning: Visit the Goethe House and Museum. Explore the life and writings of Johann Wolfgang von Goethe.

- meal: Take a leisurely meal at Cafe Hauptwache while admiring the historic setting.

- Afternoon: visit the Museum of Modern Art (MMK). The inventive displays offer a fascinating glimpse into modern art.

- Evening: Dine at Kameha Suite, which is noted for its exquisite decor and sophisticated cuisine.

Day 3: Cultural Events

- Morning: If you're going in October, start the day at the Frankfurt Book Fair. Otherwise, visit the Palmengarten, a stunning botanical garden.

- Lunch: Enjoy a meal in the Palmengarten Cafe, which offers views of the grounds.

- In the afternoon, visit the Jewish Museum Frankfurt to learn about Frankfurt's Jewish history and culture.

- Evening: Have supper at Emma Metzler, which serves a contemporary interpretation on classic German food.

Outdoor Adventure

Day 1: Hiking and Nature

- Morning: Take a short journey to the Taurus Mountains. Hike up Großer Feldberg, the range's highest summit.

- Lunch: Bring a lunch to enjoy at the peak, which offers spectacular views of the surrounding area.

- Afternoon: Wander through the magnificent paths of the Taunus Nature Park, immersing yourself in the natural splendor.

- Evening: Return to Frankfurt for supper at Lohrberg Schänke, which provides spectacular views and substantial fare.

Day 2: Water Activities

- Morning: Travel to Lake Langener Waldsee. Spend the morning windsurfing, paddleboarding, or simply resting by the ocean.

- Lunch: Have lunch at the lake's restaurant, which serves a range of dishes.

- Afternoon: Rent a bike and ride the Main Radweg (Main River Cycle Path). The well-kept route provides stunning views of the river and city.

- Evening: Return to Frankfurt for dinner at Gerbermühle, a historic restaurant with riverfront views.

Day 3: Urban Parks

- Morning: Begin the day with a visit to Nidda Park. Rent a pedal boat and explore the serene Nidda River.

- Lunch: Have a picnic in the park or go to a local cafe.

- Afternoon: Visit the Palmengarten. Wander around the themed gardens and enjoy the tranquil atmosphere.

- Evening: Wrap out your excursion with a supper at Rheinterrassen, which has breathtaking views of the Main River.

Family-friendly Trip

Day 1: Zoos and Museums.

- Morning: Begin with a visit to the Frankfurt Zoo. The range of animals and interactive exhibits are ideal for youngsters.

- Lunch: Eat in the zoo's restaurant, which has kid-friendly selections.

Afternoon: Visit the Senckenberg Natural History Museum. The dinosaur exhibitions and interactive displays are popular with youngsters.

- Evening: Have supper at Cafe Extrablatt, which serves a broad cuisine in an informal environment.

Day 2: Parks and playgrounds.

- Morning: Spend the morning at Grüneburg Park. The wide playground and open areas are ideal for family activities.

- Lunch: Pack a picnic or go to a local café.

- Afternoon: Visit the Explora Museum, an interactive science museum suitable for both children and adults.

- Dinner at Vapiano, a family-friendly restaurant that serves Italian food.

Day 3: Day trips.

- Morning: Visit the Opel Zoo in Kronberg. The zoo has interactive exhibits and gorgeous gardens.

- Lunch: Have a meal at the zoo restaurant.

- Afternoon: Return to Frankfurt and visit Nidda park. Rent a bike or pedal boat for some outdoor fun.

- Evening: Dine at Frankfurter Botschaft, which has a casual environment and a children's menu.

Budget Travel

Day 1: Free attractions.

- Morning: Begin your day with a self-guided walking trip around the Römer and Römerberg. Enjoy the architecture and history without paying a cent.

- Lunch: The Kleinmarkthalle serves quick and reasonable meals. Try the local delights at cheap costs.

- Afternoon: Visit Frankfurt Cathedral. Entry is free, while climbing the tower costs a nominal charge.

- Evening: Take a stroll along the Main River. Pack a picnic meal and watch the sunset.

Day 2: Museums and Parks

- Morning: On select days, the Städel Museum and the Museum of Modern Art (MMK) provide free admission.

- Lunch: Metzgerei Schreiber, a famous place for robust German fare, offers an economical lunch option.

- Afternoon: Spend time at the Palmengarten. The grounds are lovely, and admission is reasonably priced.

- Evening: Enjoy a low-cost supper at Der Fette Bulle, which is famed for its economical yet tasty burgers.

Day 3: Day trips and local experiences.

- Morning: Participate on a free walking tour of the city hosted by several local groups. These trips frequently include historical places and local perspectives.

- Lunch: Go to a nearby market or supermarket for a cheap dinner.

- Afternoon: Explore Eiserner Steg and Museumsufer. Many museums provide discounted admittance.

- Evening: Finish your tour with a supper at Best Worscht in Town, which is recognized for its inexpensive and delicious sausages.

Luxury Experience

Day 1: Luxury Shopping and Fine Dining.

- Morning: Begin by visiting Goethestraße, Frankfurt's top retail strip. Browse high-end retailers such as Louis Vuitton and Gucci.

- Lunch: Zenzakan is well-known for its Asian fusion food and sophisticated environment.

- Afternoon: Enjoy a spa treatment at the Jumeirah Hotel Spa. Relax and refresh in a luxury environment.

- Dinner at Restaurant Lafleur, a Michelin-starred restaurant that serves superb French food.

Day 2: Exclusive Experiences.

- Morning: Enjoy a private guided tour of the Städel Museum. Enjoy the artwork with individual thoughts.

- Lunch: Dine at Kameha Suite, which is noted for its elegant environment and delicious cuisine.

- Afternoon: Charter a private boat for a ride down the Main River. Enjoy the city skyline in elegance.

- In the evening, dine at Villa Merton, a Michelin-starred restaurant that serves inventive food in a beautiful villa.

Day 3: Day Trip and Fine Dining.

- Morning: Travel by private vehicle to the Rheingau area for a wine tasting tour. Visit well-known vineyards and enjoy special sampling.

- Lunch: Eat at a gourmet restaurant in the Rheingau, such as Schloss Johannisberg.

- Afternoon: Return to Frankfurt and browse at the Zeil and MyZeil malls.

- Evening: Finish your luxury vacation with supper at Restaurant Francais, which is famed for its outstanding French food and exceptional service.

Conclusion

Frankfurt provides a varied range of experiences for all types of travelers. Frankfurt has something for everyone, whether you're looking for a fast weekend escape, cultural immersion, outdoor experiences, a family vacation, a low-budget trip, or a luxurious experience.

Each itinerary is intended to help you make the most of your stay by emphasizing the finest that Frankfurt has to offer. These programs assure a pleasant and unforgettable visit, from touring historical monuments and appreciating world-class art to participating in outdoor activities and dining on gourmet food.

As you visit Frankfurt, take in the city's lively culture, rich history, and dynamic energy. The city's mix of old-world beauty and modern refinement produces a distinct and compelling ambiance that will leave you with lasting memories.

Have fun traveling!

CHAPTER 18

PRACTICAL INFORMATION

Planning a vacation entails more than simply selecting places and packing your belongings. To guarantee a seamless and stress-free encounter, you should come prepared with useful knowledge. During my stay in Frankfurt, I learnt a great deal about the necessities that any tourist should know. Here's a complete guide to navigating the practicalities of your trip to Frankfurt.

Currency & Banking

Frankfurt, like the rest of Germany, accepts the Euro (€) as its official currency. It's a good idea to keep extra cash on hand, especially for minor transactions and establishments that don't accept credit cards. However, most shops, restaurants, and hotels accept major credit and debit cards, such as Visa, MasterCard, and American Express.

ATMs are well distributed across the city, and I found it easy to withdraw cash as needed. Be aware that your home bank may incur costs for foreign withdrawals, so check with your bank beforehand. To avoid exorbitant costs, consider withdrawing greater amounts less frequently.

There are various currency exchange possibilities. Major banks, like Deutsche Bank, Commerzbank, and Sparkasse, provide currency exchange services. There are additional exchange bureaus positioned in strategic locations such as the airport and the main rail station. Personally, I found it easier to withdraw euros from ATMs directly.

If you want to stay in Germany for a lengthy amount of time, you may easily open a bank account. Banks such as Deutsche Bank and Commerzbank provide accounts for expats and students, frequently with English-language help.

Deutsche Bank (www.deutsche-bank.de)

Commerzbank: www.commerzbank.de.

Sparkasse: www.sparkasse.de.

Health and Medical Services

Frankfurt has high-quality health and medical services, with a large number of hospitals, clinics, and pharmacies.

It's nice to know that if you require medical care, you'll be in capable hands.

Hospitals: Frankfurt contains numerous high-quality hospitals, notably the Universitätsklinikum Frankfurt, which is linked with Goethe University. This hospital provides extensive medical services, such as emergency care, specialty treatments, and modern diagnostics. Krankenhaus Nordwest is another prominent hospital that provides excellent patient care and medical knowledge.

There are various clinics and general practitioners across the city to treat minor diseases or non-emergency circumstances. Many physicians speak English, which is helpful for non-German speakers. It is a good idea to bring your health insurance card and any other pertinent medical paperwork with you.

Pharmacies, or Apotheken, are easily accessible in Frankfurt. They are well-stocked with drugs, health items, and frequently offer basic medical advice. Look for a green cross sign. For after-hours requirements, there are 24-hour pharmacies with a rotating schedule publicized online and in pharmacy windows.

If you need prescription medicine, bring enough for the trip and keep a copy with you. If you run out, pharmacists may frequently assist you get refills, as long as you have the required documents.

Universitätsklinikum Frankfurt: www.kgu.de.

Krankenhaus Nordwest: www.krankenhaus-nordwest.de.

Pharmacy Finder: www.aponet.de

Emergency Contacts:

When traveling, it is critical to have your emergency contact numbers. Germany has a well-coordinated emergency response system, and it is necessary to be aware of the following numbers:

- 112: This is the European Union's global emergency number, which includes Germany. It allows you to contact the police, fire department, or medical emergency services.

- 110: This number is just for police emergencies.

In the event of an emergency, do not hesitate to contact these numbers. Operators usually speak various languages, including English, and will deploy the appropriate help.

Additionally, the US Consulate General in Frankfurt can be contacted for consular services, including emergency help for US citizens. It's located on Giessener Street. 30. 60435 Frankfurt am Main.

US Consulate General Frankfurt: www.de.usembassy.gov.

Internet and Connectivity

Staying connected while traveling is essential, whether for navigating the city, communicating with loved ones, or working remotely. Frankfurt provides good internet and communication possibilities.

Free Wi-Fi is frequently offered in public venues, including cafés, restaurants, shopping malls, and tourist destinations. Many hotels provide free Wi-Fi to visitors, however it is always advisable to verify the rules before booking. The Frankfurt airport also offers free Wi-Fi, which is beneficial for passengers.

SIM Cards & Mobile Data: If you want consistent internet access on the fly, consider getting a local SIM card. Major carriers such as Deutsche Telekom, Vodafone, and O2 provide prepaid SIM cards with a variety of data options. These are available in mobile phone shops, electronics stores, and even some supermarkets. I found the procedure simple, and the staff was helpful in setting up the SIM card.

Deutsche Telekom: www.telekom.de.

Vodafone Website: www.vodafone.de

O2: www.o2online.de.

Postal Services

Sending postcards, letters, or goods from Frankfurt is a straightforward and effective process. Deutsche Post is the principal postal service provider in Germany, and its services are dependable.

Post Offices: Post offices are conveniently positioned across the city and are frequently identified by a yellow sign displaying a horn symbol. They provide a variety of services, such as shipping letters and parcels, obtaining stamps, and other postal services. Many post offices also provide self-service kiosks for speedy transactions.

Mailboxes: Yellow mailboxes are located around the city, making it simple to drop off messages and postcards. Collection times are displayed on each mailbox.

International Shipping: If you need to send an item internationally, Deutsche Post and DHL (a subsidiary of Deutsche Post) provide comprehensive shipping choices. You may select from a variety of delivery speeds and services based on your preferences. DHL's express services are ideal for larger parcels or time-sensitive shipments.

Deutsche Post (www.deutschepost.de)

DHL: www.dhl.de.

Travel Insurance and Safety

Travel insurance is required for each journey, as it provides peace of mind and financial protection in the event of unforeseen circumstances. Several trustworthy firms provide comprehensive travel insurance policies that cover a wide range of scenarios, such as medical emergencies, trip cancellations, lost luggage, and more.

Choosing a Plan: When deciding on travel insurance, consider the following:

- Medical Coverage: Make sure the plan covers medical expenditures such as hospitalization, doctor visits, and prescription prescriptions.

- travel Interruption or Cancellation: Look for coverage that will compensate you for non-refundable travel expenditures if you must cancel or shorten your vacation for covered circumstances.

- Baggage and Personal Belongings: Determine if the plan covers loss, theft, or damage to your baggage and personal goods.

- 24/7 help: Many insurance companies provide round-the-clock help, which may be quite useful in an emergency.

Recommended Providers: Well-known travel insurance companies include World Nomads, Allianz Global Assistance, and AXA Travel Insurance. World Nomads provided complete coverage for my trip, and their customer support was prompt.

World Nomads (www.worldnomads.com)

Allianz Global Assistance (www.allianztravelinsurance.com)

AXA Travel Insurance (www.axa-assistance.com)

Frankfurt is typically a secure city for visitors, however it is always advisable to take normal measures. Keep your valuables safe, pay attention to your surroundings, and avoid poorly lit or abandoned locations at night. Petty crime, like as pickpocketing, can happen in crowded locations, so be cautious in places like the train station and major tourist destinations.

Final Thoughts

Having useful information at your fingertips might make your journey to Frankfurt easier and more pleasurable. Understanding the local currency and banking system, as well as knowing where to obtain medical services and staying connected with good internet, all contribute to a smooth travel experience.

Being prepared with emergency contacts and travel insurance provides an additional degree of protection, allowing you to confidently enjoy the city. With this thorough guide, you'll be well-equipped to handle the practical parts of your trip to Frankfurt, freeing up your time to enjoy everything that the city has to offer.

Have fun traveling!

CHAPTER 19

LOCAL ETIQUETTE AND CUSTOMS

Traveling to a new country is always thrilling, but it may be much more rewarding if you learn and follow local customs and manners. During my stay in Frankfurt, I made an effort to learn about the cultural norms and customs that the locals value. This chapter will help you navigate Frankfurt's social scene while ensuring that your interactions are courteous and enjoyable.

Greeting and Interaction

One of the first things I noticed about Frankfurt was the importance of greetings. When you walk into a business, restaurant, or even a tiny office, it is usual to welcome the individuals within. A simple "Guten Tag" (Good day) or "Hallo" (Hello) goes a long way toward creating a positive first impression. In more formal situations, such as business meetings, a strong handshake with eye contact is the usual welcome.

In social situations, it is courteous to address people by their titles and last names unless you are requested to use their first names. For example, you may say "Herr Müller" for Mr. Müller or "Frau Schmidt" for Mrs. Schmidt. This formality symbolizes respect and is valued in German society.

When meeting friends or close acquaintances, it is customary to exchange a brief kiss on both cheeks or a warm hug, particularly among younger people and in less formal settings. However, it is always advisable to follow the lead of your host or the person you are meeting.

Dinner Etiquette

Dining in Frankfurt, and Germany in general, has its own set of customs. When you sit down at a restaurant, it is polite to wait for everyone to be served before you begin eating. If you are asked to someone's house for a meal, bringing a little gift, such as flowers, chocolates, or a bottle of wine, is a thoughtful gesture.

When toasting, the German word "prost" is used. It is traditional to establish eye contact with each individual at the table when clinking glasses. According to mythology, this custom brings good luck and helps to prevent seven years of unpleasant sex.

Table manners are rather formal in Germany. Keep both hands visible on the table, but avoid resting your elbows. The fork is held in the left hand and the knife in the right, and it is customary to use both tools during the meal. When you're done eating, set your knife and fork parallel to your plate, pointing to the right, to indicate to the waiter that you're finished.

If you're eating in a more informal atmosphere or enjoying street cuisine, the regulations are less strict, but basic courtesy and hygiene are still expected.

Dress Code

Frankfurt is a global city with a varied population, therefore dress codes vary depending on the situation. Business dress is often formal. Men usually wear suits and ties, whilst women wear business suits or modest dresses. Frankfurt is home to numerous financial organizations, thus maintaining a professional image is essential.

Casual but tidy clothes is appropriate for everyday activities like shopping and dining out. Germans typically dress in a functional yet attractive manner. During my visit, I noted that neutral hues and well-fitted clothing were popular. Athletic apparel is often intended for sports and exercise, not casual outings.

When visiting holy places or attending formal occasions, modesty is essential. For example, if you intend to attend a church, it is appropriate to cover your shoulders and avoid wearing shorts or short skirts.

Tipping Practices

Tipping is valued in Frankfurt but not required as in other nations. In restaurants, it is typical to tip between 5 and 10% of the whole amount. Unlike in the United States, where the tip is left on the table, in Germany, the tip is given straight to the waiter when the bill is paid. For example, if your bill is €45, you might offer the waiter 50 Euro and say "Stimmt so" (keep the change).

Taxi drivers are used to rounding up their fares to the closest euro or adding a few euros. Hotel employees, like as bellhops and housekeepers, enjoy a little tip, usually 1-2 Euro per bag or per day of housekeeping services.

In pubs and cafés, it is typical to round up to the next euro or leave a little tip. If you receive excellent service, feel free to tip generously.

Public Behavior

Public demeanor in Frankfurt, like most of Germany, is restrained and courteous. Loud talking, yelling, or creating excessive noise in public areas is often considered inappropriate. Germans appreciate their personal space, thus it is courteous to keep a respectable distance whether standing in line or taking public transit.

Punctuality is very important in Germany. Whether you're seeing friends, attending a business meeting, or taking a train, arriving on time demonstrates respect and dependability. If you are running late, please tell the person you are meeting as soon as possible.

When taking public transit, it is critical to be mindful to others. Keep your voice low and avoid playing music or making phone calls. If you're wearing a backpack, please remove it and hold it in your hand or drop it on the floor to create way for other passengers.

Respecting Local Traditions

Frankfurt has a rich cultural background, and respecting local customs is an essential aspect of enjoying the city. Fasching, also known as Karneval, is a traditional event held in the run-up to Lent. During this period, you'll witness individuals dressed in spectacular costumes, parades, and other celebrations. Participating in the festivals is an excellent opportunity to immerse oneself in local culture; however, remember to be courteous and follow the example of locals.

Another tradition is the Weihnachtsmarkt (Christmas market). These markets are a valued element of German culture, taking place throughout the Advent season. When visiting a Christmas market, take the time to soak in the festive mood, eat traditional snacks like Lebkuchen (gingerbread) and Glühwein (mulled wine), and admire the artistry of the handcrafted presents and decorations for sale.

Frankfurt is well recognized for its apple wine culture. When visiting an Apfelwein pub, attempt to follow local customs like utilizing the traditional Bembel (stoneware jug) and Geripptes (ribbed glass). Joining the toast with a hearty "Prost!"" is an excellent method to interact with locals.

Environmental Guidelines

Frankfurt, like Germany as a whole, is noted for its strong dedication to environmental sustainability. Recycling and trash separation are addressed quite carefully. During my visit, I noted that garbage containers are often separated into sections for paper, plastic, glass, and miscellaneous debris. It is critical to follow these instructions and organize your waste appropriately.

Frankfurt also boasts a strong public transit infrastructure that is intended to cut carbon emissions. Using the U-Bahn (subway), S-Bahn (commuter train), trams, and buses is both convenient and ecologically friendly. Biking is another popular and environmentally beneficial method to travel about the city. There are various bike rental businesses, and the city has bike lanes and parking facilities.

Water conservation is a vital component of daily living. Germans frequently take brief showers and turn off the tap while brushing their teeth to conserve water. Energy conservation is also prioritized, with many houses and businesses utilizing energy-efficient equipment and lights.

Participating in these ecologically responsible behaviors not only demonstrates respect for local customs, but also helps to support the city's sustainability initiatives.

Conclusion

Understanding and adhering to local manners and customs may significantly improve your experience in Frankfurt. These cultural standards, which range from greeting people and dining etiquette to public behavior and environmental restrictions, let you connect with the local community and express your respect for their way of life.

Whether you're dining at a typical Apfelwein restaurant, taking part in a joyous festival, or just navigating the city's public transit system, being aware of these practices will make your visit more pleasurable and memorable. By embracing local culture and customs, you'll obtain a better grasp of what makes Frankfurt so distinctive and alive.

Have fun traveling and experiencing Frankfurt with respect and curiosity!

CHAPTER 20

WHAT TO DO AND NOT DO IN FRANKFURT

Visiting Frankfurt may be an enlightening and delightful experience provided you are aware of the local customs, safety precautions, and environmental regulations. During my stay in Frankfurt, I learnt a lot about what to do and avoid in order to have a courteous and responsible visit. This chapter will give a complete guide to navigating the do's and don'ts of visiting Frankfurt.

Local Etiquette and Customs

Do:

1. welcome People Properly: When entering a shop, restaurant, or other small place, it is customary to welcome with "Guten Tag" (Good day) or "Hallo" (Hello). When meeting someone for the first time, a solid handshake and keeping eye contact are expected.

2. Use Titles and Last Names: In formal contexts, address persons by their titles and last names unless asked to use their first name. For instance, "Frau Schmidt" or "Herr Müller".

3. Be on Time: Punctuality is highly valued in Germany. Being on time, whether for a social gathering or a business meeting, is a gesture of respect.

4. Follow Dining Etiquette: Wait until everyone has been served before beginning your meal. Keep both hands visible on the table, but avoid resting your elbows.

Don't:

1. Be Overly Familiar: Unless specifically invited, avoid addressing individuals by their first names. The usage of formal titles indicates respect.

2. Speak Loudly in Public: Germans tend to speak in moderate tones in public areas. Avoid generating too much noise or speaking loudly.

3. Ignore Personal Space: Keep a reasonable distance when dealing with others. Germans appreciate their personal space.

4. Instead of leaving tips on the table, hand them immediately to the waitress after paying the bill.

Safety Tips

Do:

1. Stay Alert: Be alert of your surroundings, particularly in congested locations such as train stations and prominent tourist attractions.

2. Use legitimate transit: Stick with legitimate taxis, public transit, or recognized ride-sharing services.

3. Keep Valuables safe: Keep your valuables close by wearing a money belt or carrying a safe bag. Frankfurt is relatively safe, however small crimes such as pickpocketing do occur.

4. Know the Emergency Numbers: In Germany, the emergency number is 112 for medical situations and 110 for police.

Don't:

1. Walk Alone at Night in unknown neighborhoods: While Frankfurt is generally secure, it is recommended to avoid wandering alone after dark in poorly lit or unknown neighborhoods.

2. Carry Large Amounts of Cash: Use credit cards or make modest cash withdrawals as required.

3. Ignore Traffic Rules: Pay special attention to pedestrian lights and crosswalks. Jaywalking is not tolerated and can result in a fine.

4. Leave stuff Unattended: Whether in a café, park, or on public transit, keep an eye on your stuff.

Environmental Guidelines

Do:

1. Recycle Properly: Separate paper, plastic, glass, and general debris into clearly designated recycling containers. Frankfurt has a strong recycling culture.

2. Conserve Water: To save water, take shorter showers and turn off the tap when brushing teeth.

3. Use Public transit: Frankfurt's public transit system is quite efficient. Using the U-Bahn, S-Bahn, trams, and buses reduces carbon emissions.

4. Participate in Local activities: If possible, attend community clean-up days or other environmental activities.

Don't:

1. Litter: Put your rubbish in the designated containers. Littering is not only unacceptable, but also punishable by fines.

2. Reduce energy waste by turning off lights and electrical gadgets when not in use. Many homes and businesses emphasize energy conservation.

3. Ignore Bike Lanes: If you're driving, be aware of the designated bike lanes and allow bicycles the right of way.

4. Use Excessive Plastic: To reduce plastic waste, choose reusable bags, bottles, and containers.

Common Tourist Mistakes

Do:

1. Learn simple German words: Knowing a few simple words, such as "Bitte" (Please), "Danke" (Thank you), and "Entschuldigung" (Excuse me), can improve your experience.

2. Plan Ahead: Look up the hours of operation for museums, restaurants, and stores. Many businesses close early on Sundays and public holidays.

3. Carry Cash: While cards are generally accepted, having some cash on hand is beneficial, especially at smaller places.

4. Respect Quiet Hours: Many residential neighborhoods have quiet hours, which range from 10 p.m. to 6 a.m. Be aware of sounds at these times.

Don't:

1. Rely only on Credit Cards: Not all locations take credit cards, particularly smaller stores and cafés.

2. Expect English Everywhere: Although many Germans know English, it is customary to begin a discussion with a German welcome.

3. Overpack: Pack lightly and comfortably, especially if you want to take public transit.

4. Ignore Local Etiquette: Simple gestures, such as greeting store employees or thanking bus drivers, go a long way toward demonstrating respect.

Respecting Local Traditions

Do:

1. Participate in Local Festivals: Enjoy the celebrations at events like as Fasching or the Christmas Market. It's an excellent approach to immerse yourself in the local culture.

2. Try Local Foods: Try traditional foods such as Grüne Soße, Handkäse, and Apfelwein. Visiting an Apfelwein tavern is essential.

3. Respect Religious places: When visiting churches or religious places, dress modestly and with respect.

4. Embrace the Local Pace: While Frankfurt might seem fast-paced, take time to relax with activities such as a walk along the Main River or a cup of coffee at a local café.

Don't:

1. Dismiss Local Customs: Understand and respect local customs, even if they differ from your own.

2. Disregard Dress Codes: In certain circumstances, such as churches or formal occasions, follow the anticipated dress code.

3. Avoid Interactions: Talk to locals and ask them about their traditions. Most individuals are eager to share their culture with you.

4. Be Impatient: Things like restaurant service may take longer. Patience is appreciated.

Tips for Responsible Travel

Do:

1. Support local businesses by eating at local restaurants, shopping at local markets, and purchasing souvenirs from local craftspeople.

2. Visit major locations during off-peak hours to avoid crowds and minimize your effect.

3. Respect Wildlife and Nature: Follow defined routes in parks and nature reserves to prevent upsetting wildlife.

4. Reduce waste by using eco-friendly products such as biodegradable toiletries and reusable water bottles.

Don't:

1. Exploit Resources: Be cautious of your utilization of water, energy, and other resources.

2. Leave a Negative Footprint: Leave things as you found them, or better. Participate in clean-ups whenever feasible.

3. Ignore Local Advice: Listen to locals for safety recommendations, environmental practices, and cultural standards.

4. Be Wasteful: Try to reduce waste by recycling, reusing, and selecting eco-friendly solutions.

Conclusion

Understanding what to do and what not to do in Frankfurt might significantly improve your vacation experience. You may have a pleasant and responsible travel by following local customs, exercising caution, and being ecologically sensitive. Avoiding frequent tourist blunders and embracing local traditions can allow you to better connect with Frankfurt's culture and people.

Whether you're meeting a local, dining at a restaurant, or touring the city's sights, these principles can help you handle your stay with ease and respect. Following these suggestions will not only make your vacation unforgettable, but it will also benefit the community and the environment.

Have fun traveling and experiencing Frankfurt with respect and curiosity!

CHAPTER 21

GREENSPACES AND PARKS

Frankfurt is well-known for its bustling financial sector and sophisticated skyline, but it also has an excellent collection of green areas and parks that provide a peaceful respite from city life. During my stay in Frankfurt, I made it a point to visit these lovely getaways, each with their own distinct charm and character. Here's a comprehensive guide to some of Frankfurt's greatest green areas and parks, ideal for a leisurely stroll, picnic, or simply appreciating nature.

Palmengarten

One of my favorite spots in Frankfurt is the Palmengarten, a breathtaking botanical garden that seems like an oasis in the heart of the city. The Palmengarten is one of Germany's largest botanical gardens, covering 22 hectares and featuring a wide array of species from throughout the world. Since its founding in 1868, the garden has been a popular attraction for both residents and tourists.

When I entered the Palmengarten, I was amazed by the diversity of themed gardens and greenhouses. The Tropicarium, a vast greenhouse complex, has a wonderful collection of tropical plants, ranging from lush ferns to towering palms. Walking into the Tropicarium seemed like entering a new universe, with the humid air and bright foliage around me.

Another feature is the Rose Garden, which bursts with color and scent during the flowering season. The well kept flower beds and graceful architecture make it ideal for a relaxing stroll or a quiet time of introspection. I particularly enjoyed the Rockery, a unique garden with alpine flora and a beautiful waterfall.

There are several seats and shaded spaces throughout the Palmengarten where you may rest and take in the scenery. The park also holds a variety of events and exhibitions throughout the year, such as concerts, plant markets, and educational programs. It's a site where you might easily spend the entire day admiring nature's magnificence.

Address: Siesmayerstraße 61, 60323 Frankfurt am Main.

Website: www.palmengarten.de.

Grüneburgpark

Grüneburgpark, located in the Westend neighborhood, is another green oasis in Frankfurt. This 29-hectare park, one of the largest in the city, provides a peaceful getaway with its wide open lawns, shady walks, and lovely flower beds. The park's name, which translates to "Green Castle Park," refers to its origins as a private garden on an aristocratic estate.

The diversity of the terrain at Grüneburgpark is one of my favorite aspects. Large meadows are ideal for picnics or frisbee, while forested parts give shade and a sense of privacy. The park's main attraction is a gorgeous lake surrounded by trees and flowers, making it ideal for a leisurely stroll or a quiet afternoon by the water.

Grüneburgpark also houses the Korean Garden, a gift from Frankfurt's sister city, Seoul. This tranquil garden has traditional Korean landscaping, such as a pond, stone lanterns, and a pavilion. It's a quiet area to sit and think, away from the noise and bustle of the city.

In addition to its natural beauty, Grüneburgpark is a popular place for residents to exercise, whether by running along the walkways, practicing yoga on the lawns, or playing sports. There are various playgrounds for children, making it an ideal location for families.

Address: August-Siebert-Straße, 60323 Frankfurt am Main.

Frankfurt City Forest

For a more immersive nature experience, the Frankfurt City Forest (Frankfurter Stadtwald) is a wonderful option. It covers over 4,800 hectares and is one of Germany's largest urban forests, providing unlimited chances for outdoor recreation and exploration. The woodland is located south of the city and is easily accessible by public transportation.

Hiking is one of my favorite hobbies in Frankfurt's City Forest. There are various well-marked routes that weave through the forest, ranging from moderate walks to strenuous excursions. The pathways lead you through a variety of environments, including thick forests, wide meadows, and tranquil ponds. One of the main attractions is the Goethe Tower, a wooden observation tower with panoramic views of the forest and the city skyline.

The forest is also a sanctuary for animals, and you're likely to see deer, foxes, and a variety of bird species throughout your stay. For birdwatchers, the forest's ponds and marshes offer excellent opportunity to see ducks and other bird species in their natural environment.

In addition to hiking, visitors to the Frankfurt City Forest enjoy cycling, equestrian riding, and picnics. There are various dedicated BBQ sites where you may eat outside. During my visit, I had a leisurely bike ride through the forest before having a picnic by one of the ponds, surrounded by the sounds of nature.

Address: Various exits in Frankfurt am Main

Website address: www.frankfurt.de.

Bethmannpark

Bethmannpark, near the busy Berger Straße, is a hidden gem of Frankfurt. This modest yet attractive park is ideal for a quiet escape from the city's hustle and bustle. Bethmannpark, which covers only 3 hectares, features wonderfully designed gardens, meandering walks, and a serene atmosphere.

One of the park's most prominent attractions is the Chinese Garden, commonly known as the Garden of Heavenly Peace. This traditional Chinese garden was designed in partnership with Frankfurt's sister city, Guangzhou, and is a stunning example of Chinese landscape architecture. The park has a pond with koi fish, a pagoda, and carefully built bridges and paths. The tranquil atmosphere and finely created features make it ideal for meditation and relaxation.

Bethmannpark also has well-kept flower beds, a rose garden, and a few statues and sculptures that add to its ambiance. During my visit, I liked relaxing on one of the numerous seats, reading a book, and taking in the serene surroundings. The park's small size makes it easy to explore, and it's an excellent location to relax after a long day.

Address: Friedberger Landstraße 8, 60316 Frankfurt am Main.

Günthersburgpark

Günthersburgpark, located in the Nordend area, is a popular spot for families and outdoor lovers. This 7-hectare park contains a range of leisure facilities, such as playgrounds, sports fields, and open areas for picnics and relaxing. The park's colorful environment and numerous amenities make it a popular place among residents.

One of the attractions of Günthersburgpark is its enormous playground, which has a range of equipment for children of all ages. There are climbing structures, swings, slides, and even a water play area for those hot summer days. The playground is well-kept and provides a secure and enjoyable space for children to play and explore.

The park also features basketball courts, soccer fields, and a skate park. During my stay, I liked attending a local soccer game and seeing the skate park packed with eager skaters. The expansive grounds are ideal for a game of frisbee or simply lounging in the grass and enjoying the weather.

In addition to its recreational amenities, Günthersburgpark has lovely gardens and shady paths. The park's center fountain and surrounding flower beds provide a magnificent backdrop for a leisurely stroll. There are various picnic sites with tables and seats, making it an excellent choice for a family excursion.

Address: Hartmann-Ibach-Straße, 60389 Frankfurt am Main.

Nizza Park

Nizza Park, located on the banks of the Main River, features a unique combination of Mediterranean and native vegetation. This 4-hectare park is recognized for its mild microclimate, which allows a wide range of Mediterranean flora to thrive. The park's unique ambiance and riverbank location make it ideal for a quiet stroll or leisurely day.

One of my favorite aspects of Nizza Park was its rich plant life. Palm palms, fig trees, and other Mediterranean species lend the park its particular character. Walking around the park, I felt as if I had been transported to another universe, surrounded by lush foliage and the soothing murmur of the river.

Nizza Park also has various walking pathways and lots of seats to sit and enjoy the scenery. The park's location along the Main River affords breathtaking views of both the river and the city skyline. It's a popular area for folks to walk, exercise, or just rest by the river.

During the summer months, the park's shady spaces and fresh breezes provide an ideal respite from the heat. I liked taking a lunch and spending the day reading a book while watching the boats pass by on the river.

Address: Untermainkai 60329 Frankfurt am Main.

Lohrpark

Lohrpark, located atop the Lohrberg, is one of Frankfurt's highest points and provides stunning views of the city and surrounding area. Lohrpark, which spans 17 hectares, is a favorite location for both residents and visitors looking for a picturesque and tranquil escape.

One of the park's primary attractions is the panoramic viewpoint, which offers breathtaking views of Frankfurt's cityscape, the primary River, and the Taunus Mountains in the distance. The vista is especially picturesque around sunset, when the city is drenched in golden light. During my visit, I spent a pleasant evening at the overlook, admiring the gorgeous surroundings and enjoying the cold wind.

Lohrpark also houses a vineyard, one of the few within the municipal borders. The vineyard produces local wine, which may be tasted at the park's wine bar, Lohrberg Schänke. The pub has outside seating with stunning views of the vineyard and the city, making it an ideal place to enjoy a glass of wine and traditional German food.

The park has well-kept walking routes, picnic spots, and playgrounds, making it an excellent choice for families. There are also various BBQ places where you may cook and share a meal with friends and family. During my visit, I noticed many families having picnics and barbecues, which created a vibrant and inviting ambiance.

Address: Huthparkweg 1, 60389 Frankfurt am Main.

Conclusion

Frankfurt's green areas and parks provide a wide variety of natural beauty and leisure activities. Whether you're exploring the exotic flora of Palmengarten, having a family adventure in Günthersburgpark, or admiring the panoramic views of Lohrpark, there's a park for every mood and occasion.

These green getaways provide an ideal break from the city, enabling you to rest, relax, and reconnect with nature. Each park has its own distinct charm and character, providing something distinctive for every visitor. As you explore these lovely locations, take time to appreciate the peace and beauty that Frankfurt's parks have to offer.

Happy exploring!

CHAPTER 22

UNIQUE EXPERIENCES

Aside from its renowned skyline and bustling business center, Frankfurt offers a variety of unique experiences. There's always something interesting to explore, from tranquil river cruises and fine wine excursions to engaging culinary lessons and exciting art tours. I've spent a large amount of time in Frankfurt and have had the privilege of participating in some genuinely unusual events, which I strongly suggest. Here's a full introduction to some of the most memorable and unique experiences available in Frankfurt.

River Cruises Along the Main

One of the greatest ways to admire Frankfurt's beautiful skyline and lovely surroundings is to take a river boat along the Main River. These cruises provide a relaxing and picturesque opportunity to experience the city from a new viewpoint.

Day Cruises: During the day, you may take a number of sightseeing cruises down the river, which provide panoramic views of Frankfurt's monuments. I took a cruise with Primus-Linie, which provided a complete tour of the city's waterfront. The boat passed by famous landmarks including the Eiserner Steg (Iron Bridge), the massive ECB building, and the beautiful greenery of Nizza Park. The onboard commentary gave valuable information on the history and significance of these places.

Evening cruises provide a more romantic and wonderful experience. As the sun sets, the city lights begin to shine, providing a stunning vista. I especially enjoyed the evening dinner cruise. It was a delightful and private event, complete with great cuisine, quiet music, and Frankfurt's stunning nightscape.

Specialty Cruises: Themed cruises, such as wine sampling or jazz cruises, combine sightseeing with unique cultural activities. These specialty cruises are an excellent chance to sample local cuisine and entertainment while taking in the scenery.

Primus Line: www.primus-linie.de.

Wine Tours throughout the surrounding region

Frankfurt is ideally positioned near some of Germany's most well-known wine areas, making it an ideal location for wine excursions. The surrounding Rheingau and Rheinhessen districts are well-known for their superb wines, notably Rieslings.

Rheingau Wine Tour: The Rheingau area, which runs along the Rhine River, is famed for its scenic vineyards, ancient wineries, and lovely villages. I took a guided tour that included stops at notable vineyards like Schloss Johannisberg and Kloster Eberbach. At each winery, I was able to visit the vineyards, learn about the winemaking process, and, of course, drink a range of delicious wines. The journey also included a visit to the lovely town of Rüdesheim, where I explored the tiny alleys lined with wine pubs and ate traditional cuisine.

Rheinhessen Wine Tour: Another excellent choice is the Rheinhessen region, which is Germany's largest wine-producing area. The undulating hills and excellent soil provide optimal growing conditions for a diverse selection of grape types. I went on a tour to several family-owned vineyards, where I sampled everything from delicate Rieslings to strong Spätburgunders. The winemakers were extremely enthusiastic and knowledgable, making the trip both instructive and fun.

Booking Tips: Many tour companies provide day tours from Frankfurt to these wine areas that include transportation, tastings, and lunches. Booking in advance is recommended, especially during high tourist season.

Schloss Johannisberg (www.schloss-johannisberg.de)

Kloster Eberbach (www.kloster-eberbach.de)

Cooking Classes and Food Tours

Consider taking a cooking class or going on a food tour in Frankfurt to get some hands-on culinary experience. These events are an excellent way to immerse yourself in the local cuisine culture while learning new skills.

Cooking Classes: I took a cooking class at Cooking Time, where I learned how to make classic German foods like sauerbraten (marinated pot roast) and apfelstrudel. The session was given by a kind and skilled chef who walked us through every step, from choosing fresh ingredients to perfecting culinary methods. At the end of the lesson, we ate the beautiful dinner we had cooked, complimented by local wine.

Food Tours: Frankfurt's culinary scene is rich and active, and a food tour is a fantastic way to experience it. I went on a culinary trip with Frankfurt culinary Tours, which took us through the lively Kleinmarkthalle and stylish Sachsenhausen quarter. We tried a variety of local favorites, such as Handkäse mit Musik (cheese with onions), Grüne Soße (green sauce), and freshly made pretzels. The tour also featured stops at hidden jewels such as family-owned bakeries and artisanal chocolate businesses.

Cooking Time (www.cookingtime.de)

Frankfurt Food Tours (www.frankfurtfoodtours.de)

Hidden gems and offbeat attractions

Frankfurt is rich with hidden jewels and unusual sights that provide a distinct perspective on the city's character and history. These lesser-known destinations are ideal for daring tourists wishing to venture beyond the typical tourist route.

Dialog Museum: One of the most amazing experiences I had was visiting the Dialog Museum, which features a series of interactive displays that imitate the sensation of blindness. Visitors are guided by sight challenged hosts through entirely darkness rooms, depending solely on their other senses. The event was both eye-opening and thought-provoking, offering a better understanding of the difficulties experienced by visually challenged people.

Explora Museum: The Explora Museum is another unique sight worth seeing. This interactive science museum houses a number of displays that investigate optical illusions, holography, and other visual phenomena. It's a pleasant and instructive experience for people of all ages, and I loved trying out the hands-on displays.

Kleinmarkthalle: For a sense of local life, stop by the Kleinmarkthalle, a lively indoor market where merchants sell fresh fruit, meats, cheeses, and specialty dishes. It's a terrific spot to try local cuisine, buy unusual gifts, and mingle with friendly locals. I enjoyed walking through the aisles, sampling samples, and talking with merchants about their products.

Dialog Museum (www.dialogmuseum.de)

Explora Museum website: www.explora.info.

Art and Graffiti Tours

Frankfurt's art culture is diversified and active, combining conventional galleries with vivid street art. Joining an art or graffiti tour is a great opportunity to discover the city's artistic side.

Frankfurt has numerous world-class art galleries, notably the Städel Museum and the Museum of Modern Art (MMK). I had a guided tour that presented in-depth insights into the museums' collections, including major pieces by Rembrandt, Monet, and Picasso. The tour also included visits to smaller, independent galleries that featured current and experimental art.

Graffiti Tours: To gain an alternative viewpoint, I joined a graffiti tour with Alternative Frankfurt Tours. The journey took us through the Bahnhofsviertel and Ostend districts, where we saw colorful street art and graffiti artwork. Our guide, a local artist, told us amazing tales about the painters and the significance of their work. It was an eye-opening encounter that exposed a vibrant and sometimes neglected side of Frankfurt's culture.

Städel Museum (www.staedelmuseum.de)

Museum of Modern Art (MMK) website: www.mmk-frankfurt.de

Alternative Frankfurt Tours (www.alternativefrankfurt.com)

Local Markets and Artisanal Workshops

Frankfurt's neighborhood markets and artisan workshops provide a fantastic opportunity to explore unique goods and learn traditional skills.

Bornheimer Wochenmarkt: One of my favorite neighborhood markets is the Bornheimer Wochenmarkt, which takes place every Wednesday and Saturday. This beautiful market has a diverse selection of vendors providing fresh fruit, artisanal cheeses, baked delicacies, and handcrafted crafts. It's an excellent spot to get picnic materials or buy unusual presents. I loved interacting with the sellers and learning about their items, which ranged from organic veggies to handcrafted soaps.

Artisan Workshops: For a hands-on experience, try attending an artisan workshop. I took a pottery session at Keramikwerkstatt Noe, where I studied the fundamentals of pottery and made my own ceramic item. The session was taught by a competent artisan who gave individual training and imparted knowledge about the technique. It was a satisfying experience to make something with my own hands and bring it home as a one-of-a-kind keepsake.

Bornheimer Wochenmarkt: At the Berger Straße, 60316 Frankfurt am Main.

Keramikwerkstatt Noe (www.keramikwerkstatt-noe.de)

Seasonal Activities & Events

Frankfurt presents a range of seasonal activities and events that provide unique experiences all year. These events provide an excellent opportunity to immerse yourself in local culture while also enjoying the city's festive atmosphere.

The Frankfurt Christmas Market, which runs from late November to December in the Römerberg and Paulsplatz, is one of the holiday season's highlights. The market has attractively adorned kiosks selling homemade products, Christmas meals, and mulled wine. I enjoyed meandering through the market, seeing the dazzling lights, and trying goodies such as roasted chestnuts and gingerbread.

The Frankfurt Apple Wine Festival takes place during the summer and celebrates the city's favorite drink, Apfelwein (apple wine). The event takes place at the Roßmarkt and showcases a range of apple wines from local producers, as well as traditional food, music, and dancing. It's a colorful and enjoyable event that gives visitors a taste of Frankfurt's cultural legacy.

The Opernplatz Festival, held in June, transforms the area in front of the Alte Oper into a lively outdoor arena. The event includes live music, shows, and a variety of food and beverage kiosks. The balmy summer evenings and picturesque backdrop make for a memorable experience.

Frankfurt Christmas Market website: www.frankfurt-tourismus.de.

Frankfurt Apple Wine Festival (www.frankfurt-tourismus.de)

Opernplatz Festival (www.opernplatzfest.de)

Conclusion

Frankfurt has a plethora of unique experiences that go beyond the usual tourist attractions. The city offers a variety of activities to explore and experience, including calm river cruises and educational wine excursions, as well as vivid art and graffiti tours.

Whether you're taking a cooking class, exploring local markets, or visiting seasonal festivals, these one-of-a-kind activities give you a better understanding of Frankfurt's culture and character. Each activity allows you to explore the city from a unique angle, making your vacation genuinely unforgettable.

As you enjoy these one-of-a-kind experiences, remember to admire the creativity, history, and traditions that make Frankfurt such a vibrant and engaging city. These experiences will not only enhance your vacation experience, but will also provide you with lasting memories of this amazing city.

Happy exploring!

CONCLUSION

1. RECAP OF FRANKFURT HIGHLIGHTS

As my time in Frankfurt comes to a conclusion, I find myself reminiscing on the diverse experiences that this lively city has provided. Frankfurt, with its distinct combination of old-world charm and modern refinement, has grabbed me in ways I did not expect. From the renowned skyline dominated by towering buildings to the beautiful green spaces that provide a peaceful respite, every region of Frankfurt has something unique to offer.

Historical structures like the Römer and Frankfurt Cathedral have made me appreciate the city's rich legacy. Walking around these old places, I felt a genuine connection to the past, as if the ghosts of history were whispering their tales. Cultural institutions such as the Städel Museum and the Museum of Modern Art (MMK) have demonstrated Frankfurt's dedication to conserving and promoting art in all forms.

The lively communities, each with its own distinct personality, gave layers of variety to my trip. Exploring the fashionable cafés and shops of Sachsenhausen, the busy market stalls of Kleinmarkthalle, and the tranquil serenity of Palmengarten provided a comprehensive picture of daily life in Frankfurt. The gastronomic pleasures, ranging from traditional German meals to foreign cuisine, enticed my taste buds and introduced me to sensations I'll never forget.

2. Travelers' Reflections and Testimonials

As a traveler who has spent a substantial amount of time in Frankfurt, I can say that the city has made a lasting impression on me. From the minute I arrived, the villagers greeted me with warmth and friendliness. Whether I was asking for directions or having a simple discussion at a café, Frankfurt residents were always ready to share their city with me.

One unforgettable event was doing a wine tour across the Rheingau area. The undulating vineyards, the history of the wineries, and the excellent taste of the wines all left an impression. It was a day full of laughing, learning, and the excitement of meeting new people. Another highlight was the evening river trip on the Main, with the city lights reflecting on the water creating a magnificent atmosphere. These moments, among many more, have made my time in Frankfurt very memorable.

Fellow passengers' testimonials mirror my feelings. Sarah, a fellow traveler, said, "Frankfurt exceeded my expectations." My stay was made unforgettable by the combination of history and contemporary, the great cuisine, and the nice people. I cannot wait to return!" Another tourist, John, said, "The art and cultural scene in Frankfurt is outstanding." I enjoyed the museums and street art excursions. It's a city that fosters innovation.

3. Tips for Your Next Visit

If you're considering a vacation to Frankfurt, here are some recommendations to help you make the most of your stay:

1. Plan ahead of time: Look up the locations you wish to visit and confirm their hours of operation. Many museums and attractions have set days when they are closed or have limited hours.

2. Use Public Transportation: Frankfurt has a fantastic public transportation system. The U-Bahn, S-Bahn, trams, and buses provide easy and efficient transportation around the city.

3. Learn Basic German words: While many people in Frankfurt speak English, learning a few basic German words such as "Bitte" (Please), "Danke" (Thank you), and "Entschuldigung" (Excuse me) might help make your encounters go more smoothly and fun.

4. Explore Different Neighborhoods: Every area in Frankfurt has its own distinct atmosphere. Spend time in

places like Sachsenhausen, Bornheim, and Westend to gain a sense of the local culture.

5. Try Local Cuisine: Don't skip classic delicacies like Grüne Soße, Handkäse, and Apfelwein. For a really genuine gastronomic experience, visit local markets and family-owned eateries.

6. Participate in events & Events: Frankfurt holds several events throughout the year. Whether it's the Frankfurt Book Fair, the Christmas Market, or the Apple Wine Festival, these events are excellent opportunities to immerse yourself in local culture.

4. Staying connected with Frankfurt

Even when you leave Frankfurt, there are various methods to stay in touch with the city and keep your memories alive:

1. Follow Local Social Media Pages: Many Frankfurt museums, cultural institutions, and tourist sites have active social media accounts. Follow them to stay up to date on city events, exhibits, and news.

2. Join Online Communities: There are various online communities and forums where Frankfurt travelers may share their experiences, recommendations, and travel anecdotes. Joining these communities might help you connect with other visitors and locals.

3. Subscribe to Newsletters: Many tourism websites and cultural organizations give newsletters with information

about forthcoming events, travel suggestions, and fascinating articles about Frankfurt.

4. Stay in Touch with Friends: If you made friends during your visit, keep in touch with them. They can keep you up to speed on what's going on in the city and may even help you plan your next visit.

5. Plan a Return Trip: There is always more to discover in Frankfurt. Planning a return trip might offer you something to look forward to while also deepening your relationship with the place.

5. Final words and farewell

As I complete my adventure in Frankfurt, I am overwhelmed with appreciation for the experiences and memories I have gained. Frankfurt is a city that provides far more than meets the eye. It's a location where history and modernity coexist peacefully, multiple cultures merge perfectly, and every corner contains a tale waiting to be explored.

My stay in Frankfurt has been a journey of discovery, with moments of astonishment, learning, and connection. From the busy streets of the financial sector to the serene walkways of its parks, every aspect of the city has made an indelible imprint on me. The art, food, people, and bright spirit of Frankfurt have all contributed to a wonderful journey.

As I leave Frankfurt, I take with me not just memories, but also a new appreciation for the city's vast tapestry of experiences. Dear reader, I advise you to discover Frankfurt with an open heart and an inquisitive mind. Accept its distinct charm, savor its gastronomic pleasures, and immerse yourself in its cultural heritage. Whether it's your first visit or one of many, Frankfurt always welcomes you back with open arms and fresh adventures.

Thank you, Frankfurt, for the beautiful memories and many moments of delight. Until we meet again, Auf Wiedersehen!

Enjoy your travels!

APPENDIX

USEFUL RESOURCES

Traveling to a new place may be both thrilling and intimidating. Having the correct resources at your disposal may make your experience easier and more pleasurable. During my time in Frankfurt, I discovered numerous excellent tools to help me navigate the city, remain secure, and learn more about its rich culture. Here's a complete list of useful resources to help you make the most of your trip to Frankfurt.

Emergency Contacts

Knowing the emergency contact numbers is essential while traveling to a new location. Frankfurt, like the rest of Germany, has a well-integrated emergency response system. Here are the crucial numbers you should have handy:

1. The general emergency number (police, fire, and ambulance) is 112.

- This is the emergency number for the whole European Union, including Germany. You can call this number to reach the police, fire department, or medical emergency services. Operators generally speak several languages, including English.

2. Police non-emergency number: 110.

- Call this number in non-emergency circumstances that nevertheless require police intervention.

3. Medical Assistance:

- Universitätsklinikum Frankfurt (The University Hospital Frankfurt):

Address: Theodor-Stern-Kai 7, 60590 Frankfurt am Main.

- Website: www.kgu.de.

- Krankenhaus Nordwest, or Northwest Hospital:

- Address: Steinbacher Hohl 2–26, 60488 Frankfurt am Main

- Website address: www.krankenhaus-nordwest.de

4. Pharmacies:

Apotheken-Notdienst (Pharmacy Emergency Service)

- Website address: www.aponet.de

- This website lists the nearest open pharmacies, including those open after hours.

5. US Consulate General in Frankfurt:

- Address: Giessener Street. 30, 60435 Frankfurt am Main.

Having these contacts saved on your phone may give you piece of mind and guarantee you're ready for any occasion.

Maps and Navigation Tools

Navigating a new city might be difficult, but with the correct maps and tools, it gets significantly simpler. Here are some tools that I found really useful for navigating Frankfurt:

1. Google maps:

- Site: www.google.com/maps.

- Google Maps is an indispensable tool for navigating. It offers precise maps and instructions for driving, walking, cycling, and taking public transit, as well as real-time traffic updates. I used Google Maps extensively to navigate the city and explore surrounding activities and eateries.

2. Frankfurt Tourism Map:

- Website address: www.frankfurt-tourismus.de

- The official tourist website provides downloadable maps and guides highlighting major sights, public transit routes, and walking tours. These maps are very handy for arranging your schedule and ensuring you don't miss any major attractions.

3. The Rhein-Main-Verkehrsverbund (RMV) app:

- Website: www.rmv.de.

- This app is essential for navigating the Frankfurt public transit system. It lists timetables, routes, and ticket prices for the U-Bahn, S-Bahn, trams, and buses. The app also provides real-time notifications on delays and service changes.

4. Offline maps:

- Consider downloading offline maps using programs such as Google Maps or Maps.me. This is especially beneficial if you're concerned about data use or find yourself in a region with limited internet access.

Having these navigational tools at your disposal will let you explore Frankfurt more efficiently and without worry.

Additional Reading and References

To really understand Frankfurt's rich history and dynamic culture, I recommend doing some more reading and research. These materials give a fuller understanding of the city's tradition, architecture, and recent advancements.

1. Lonely Planet's "Frankfurt: City Guide"

- This thorough handbook includes complete information about Frankfurt's sights, eating, shopping, and lodging alternatives. It also offers useful information and maps to help you navigate the city.

2. "Frankfurt Then and Now" by Carola Nathan

- This book offers a fascinating look into Frankfurt's evolution over time, with side-by-side images contrasting historical and modern perspectives of the city. It's an excellent resource for history fans and anybody interested in urban development.

3. Frankfurt Tourism's Website:

- Website address: www.frankfurt-tourismus.de

- The official tourist website has a wealth of information, including guides, itineraries, event calendars, and travel recommendations. It's a great place to start when it comes to arranging your trip and learning about the city's attractions.

4. Goethe Institute Frankfurt:

- Website: www.goethe.de/frankfurt.

- The Goethe-Institut provides cultural activities, language classes, and information about German culture and literature. It's an excellent location to learn more about Frankfurt's cultural scene and hone your German abilities.

5. "Frankfurt: A Cultural Guide" by Jens Burkhard

- This guidebook focuses on Frankfurt's cultural landmarks, museums, galleries, and theaters. It offers insights into the city's cultural and intellectual life, making it an invaluable resource for culture lovers.

Useful Local Phrases

While many Frankfurt residents understand English, learning a few basic German words can improve your trip experience and allow you to engage with locals. Here are a few phrases that I found extremely useful:

1. Greetings and Polite Expressions:

   - Hallo! (Hello!)

   - Guten Morgen! (Good morning!)

   - Guten Tag! (Good day!)

   - Guten Abend! (Good evening!)

   - Auf Wiedersehen! (Goodbye!)

   - Bitte. (Please.)

   - Danke. (Thank you.)

   - Entschuldigung. (Excuse me.)

2. Basic Questions:

   - Wie geht es Ihnen? (How are you?)

   - Sprechen Sie Englisch? (Do you speak English?)

   - Wo ist die nächste U-Bahn-Station? (Where is the nearest subway station?)

   - Wie viel kostet das? (How much does this cost?)

   - Können Sie mir helfen? (Can you help me?)

   - Wo ist das Badezimmer? (Where is the bathroom?)

3. Dining and Shopping:

   - Ich hätte gerne... (I would like…)

   - Die Speisekarte, bitte. (The menu, please.)

- Kann ich die Rechnung haben? (Can I have the bill?)

- Haben Sie... (Do you have…)

- Wie spät ist es? (What time is it?)

4. Emergency Phrases:

- Ich brauche Hilfe. (I need help.)

- Rufen Sie die Polizei. (Call the police.)

- Ich bin verletzt. (I am injured.)

- Wo ist das Krankenhaus? (Where is the hospital?)

Having these words on hand can help to make your encounters run more smoothly and pleasurable. It demonstrates respect for the local culture and can help you negotiate a variety of circumstances more efficiently.

Conclusion

Having the correct materials and knowledge may really improve your trip experience in Frankfurt. From emergency contacts and navigational tools to supplemental reading and essential words, being well-prepared assures a smooth and pleasurable trip.

Frankfurt is a city of contrasts and surprises, where modernism and history coexist, and urban life easily combines with natural beauty. By employing these materials, you will be able to confidently navigate the city, have a better grasp of its rich cultural legacy, and engage more deeply with its residents.

Whether you're visiting the historic Römer, taking a peaceful stroll through Palmengarten, or finding hidden treasures in the city's colorful districts, these tools will help you make the most of your stay in Frankfurt.

Thank you for accompanying me on my adventure across Frankfurt. I hope you found this tutorial helpful and motivating. Safe travels and great exploration!

Auf Wiedersehen!

Addresses and Locations for Popular Accommodation

Frankfurt has a wide selection of lodgings to satisfy any traveler's preferences, from opulent hotels to low-cost options and distinctive boutique stays. The following are some of the most popular locations to stay in the city:

1. Jumeirah Frankfurt, Thurn-und-Taxis-Platz 2, 60313 Frankfurt am Main. Website: www.jumeirah.com.

   - Jumeirah Frankfurt is located in the center of Frankfurt and provides magnificent accommodations with panoramic city views, a full-service spa, and outstanding dining options. It's an excellent choice for tourists wanting both comfort and elegance.

2. Steigenberger Frankfurter Hof, located at Am Kaiserplatz, 60311 Frankfurt am Main, has a website at www.steigenberger.com.

- This beautiful hotel has represented luxury since 1876. With its strategic position between the business sector and the Römer, the Steigenberger Frankfurter Hof combines historic elegance with modern conveniences.

3. Fleming's Hotel, Frankfurt Main-Riverside

- Location: Langestraße 5-9, 60311 Frankfurt am Main - Website: www.flemings-hotels.com

- Fleming's Hotel is known for its modern style and great service. It is located near the Main River and provides convenient access to Frankfurt's main attractions. The hotel has spacious rooms, a fitness facility, and a sophisticated restaurant.

4. 25hours Hotel The Goldman - Location: Hanauer Landstraße 127, 60314 Frankfurt am Main - Website: www.25hours-hotels.com This stylish boutique hotel in the Ostend neighborhood is noted for its unique design and lively environment. Each room is artistically furnished, and the hotel's restaurant, Goldman Restaurant, is a favorite hangout for both visitors and residents.

5. Motel One Frankfurt-Römer - Address: Berliner Straße 55, 60311 Frankfurt am Main - Website: www.motel-one.com.

- Motel One is a wonderful choice for budget-conscious tourists, offering modern, attractive rooms at reasonable prices. Its strategic position in the Römer and commercial sector gives it an excellent starting point for exploring the city.

Addresses and Locations of Popular Restaurants and Cafes

Frankfurt's food scene is diversified and active, ranging from traditional German cuisine to foreign delicacies. Here are some of the city's popular eateries and cafes:

1. Apfelwein Wagner - Address: Schweizer Straße 71, 60594 Frankfurt am Main - Website: www.apfelwein-wagner.com.

- Apfelwein Wagner, located in the Sachsenhausen neighborhood, is well-known for its traditional apple wine and robust German cuisine. It's a terrific location to learn about local culinary traditions in a pleasant, rustic atmosphere.

2. Main Tower Restaurant & Lounge - Location: Neue Mainzer Straße 52-58, 60311 Frankfurt am Main - Website: www.maintower-restaurant.de

- This restaurant, located on the 53rd story of the Main Tower, provides stunning views of the city skyline as well as a refined menu of European cuisine. It's ideal for a nice evening out.

3. Dauth-Schneider - Address: Neuer Wall 5-7, 60594 Frankfurt am Main - Website: www.dauth-schneider.de.

- Dauth-Schneider, another renowned restaurant in Sachsenhausen, provides classic Frankfurt dishes such as Handkäse mit Musik and Grüne Soße. On a hot day, the restaurant's beer garden is the ideal location to unwind.

4. Kleinmarkthalle location: Hasengasse 5-7, 60311 Frankfurt am Main. This lively indoor market is a foodie's dream, featuring a diverse selection of fresh fruit, meats, cheeses, and specialty delicacies. Grab a snack at one of the market's many food vendors and soak in the vibrant ambiance.

5. Cafe Hauptwache - Address: An der Hauptwache 15, 60313 Frankfurt am Main - Located in the city center, this historic café is a popular destination for breakfast, lunch, or coffee breaks. Its patio has excellent views of the Hauptwache square, making it an ideal spot to people-watch.

Addresses and Locations of Popular Bars and Clubs

Frankfurt's nightlife is busy and diverse, ranging from quaint taverns to contemporary nightclubs. The following are some of the city's most popular pubs and clubs:

1. Jimmy's Bar - Location: Friedrich-Ebert-Anlage 40, 60325 Frankfurt am Main Jimmy's Bar, housed in the Grandhotel Hessischer Hof, is a traditional cocktail bar with a classy environment. It's the ideal place for a refined night out, with great beverages and live piano music.

2. Gibson Club - Location: Zeil 85-93, 60313 Frankfurt am Main - Website: www.gibson-club.de Gibson Club, one of Frankfurt's most popular nightclubs, is known for its live music and DJ sets. The club's modern design and dynamic ambiance draw a fashionable audience wanting to party the night away.

3. The Kinly Bar - Location: Elbestraße 34, 60329 Frankfurt am Main This speakeasy-style pub in the Bahnhofsviertel neighborhood is famous for its inventive drinks and small setting. The educated bartenders create bespoke beverages based on your tastes.

4. O'Reilly's Irish Pub - Location: Am Hauptbahnhof 4, 60329 Frankfurt am Main - Website: www.oreillys.com

- O'Reilly's is a popular among both locals and foreigners, with a vibrant environment, substantial pub cuisine, and a diverse beer selection. It's an excellent venue for watching a sporting event or listening to live music.

5. Club Travolta - Address: Brönnerstraße 17, 60313 Frankfurt am Main - A popular nightclub with two dance floors and many music genres, including house, techno, hip-hop, and R&B. The club's lively atmosphere and talented DJs make it a must-see for nightlife fans.

Addresses and Locations of the Top Attractions

Frankfurt is a city steeped in history, culture, and modern attractions. Here are some of the best websites you won't want to miss:

1. Römer & Römerberg

- Location: Römerberg 27, 60311 Frankfurt am Main. - Website: www.frankfurt-tourismus.de. The Römer is Frankfurt's medieval municipal hall, situated on the scenic Römerberg Square. This region is a must-see for its stunning medieval buildings and lively atmosphere.

2. Frankfurt Cathedral (Kaiserdom St. Bartholomäus): Domplatz 1, 60311 Frankfurt am Main. Website: www.dom-frankfurt.de.

- The Gothic cathedral is one of Frankfurt's most important historical sites. Climb the tower to get panoramic views of the city.

3. Städel Museum - Address: Schaumainkai 63, 60596 Frankfurt am Main - Website: www.staedelmuseum.de The Städel Museum, one of Germany's most prominent art museums, includes a large collection of European art dating from the Middle Ages to the present.

4. Palmengarten - Location: Siesmayerstraße 61, 60323 Frankfurt am Main - Website: www.palmengarten.de This enormous botanical park has a broad array of plants from throughout the world, as well as exquisite themed gardens and greenhouses.

5. Goethe House is located at Großer Hirschgraben 23-25, 60311 Frankfurt am Main and has a website at www.goethehaus-frankfurt.de. This museum, located in Johann Wolfgang von Goethe's birthplace, provides an intriguing look into the life and work of Germany's greatest writer.

6. Main Tower - Location: Neue Mainzer Straße 52-58, 60311 Frankfurt am Main - Website: www.maintower.de The observation deck of the Main Tower offers the greatest

views of Frankfurt's skyline. It provides a 360-degree perspective of the city and beyond.

7. Senckenberg Natural History Museum, located at Senckenberganlage 25, 60325 Frankfurt am Main, has a website at www.senckenberg.de. This museum is popular among families and natural history aficionados, with large exhibits on dinosaurs, fossils, and biodiversity.

These addresses and places should help you navigate Frankfurt and make the most of your stay, ensuring that you see the most that the city has to offer. Happy exploring!

Printed in Great Britain
by Amazon